I0137084

GRATITUDE
AND GOALS

CREATE THE LIFE YOU WOULD LOVE TO LIVE

GRATITUDE AND GOALS

STACEY GREWAL

Foreword by Paul J. Meyer
New York Times Bestselling Author of *Dynamics of Personal Goal Setting*

CREATE THE LIFE YOU WOULD LOVE TO LIVE

GRATITUDE AND GOALS

All rights reserved
Copyright © 2010 Stacey Grewal

Cover design by Tara Mayberry
Interior design by Ted Ruybal.

All rights reserved. No part of this publication may be reproduced or transmitted
in any form or by any means, electronic or mechanical, including
photocopy, recording, or any information storage and retrieval system,
without permission in writing from the publisher. Printed in the United States
of America.

ISBN:13 978-0-615-29877-1
LCCN: 2010902347
First Edition
1 2 3 4 5 6 7 8 9 10

For information, please visit:
www.gratitudeandgoals.com
www.staceygrewal.com

CONTENTS

BOOK ONE

You Are the Master of Your Today
and the Creator of Your Tomorrow

BOOK TWO

It's Time To Take Action

If you had a choice to live the life you're living now or the life you've always dreamed of, which one would you choose? The choice is yours . . .

FOREWORD

Paul J. Meyer

Stacey Grewal has a passion. I can appreciate people with passion. They are the ones with a singular purpose and dogged determination that can make a difference in this chaotic, sometimes all-consuming world. But what intrigued me the most about Stacey and her book, *Gratitude and Goals*, is that she combined two topics about which I, too, am passionate.

Gratitude is something so many of us have just plain forgotten about. I may be showing my age here, although it's no secret I've lived on this earth long enough to speak from experience, but I remember being frequently admonished by my parents to be grateful for *everything*—even during the most difficult of times. Actually, it's during the tough times that we need to be most grateful because I can assure you, there will always be someone in a worse situation. More importantly, a lack of gratitude leads to self-pity which is a particularly debilitating and self-defeating attitude. It can plunge you so far into the abyss that it's difficult to ever see the "bright side" of life.

This is the very idea Stacey so honestly conveys throughout her book. Faced with a series of life-altering challenges, she admits to succumbing to the abyss—"a deep-cycle of self-pity, resentment, and blame." Then, she reached her personal epiphany. This insight, which she gives credit to God for revealing to her (Belief in The Almighty is another shared passion, by the way), was to *"Change your way of thinking and behaving . . . Positive thought reaps positive reward . . . Gratitude is the key!"*

Newly energized, Stacey set out to make an attitude of gratitude the focus of her life. This is where another shared passion comes into play. Having experienced the power of goal setting while working in a corporate environment, Stacey discovered an unbeatable formula: Gratitude + Goals = *SUCCESS*.

I won't reveal exactly why Stacey's formula works—you'll have to read her book to find that out for yourself; but for someone who has been a life-long student (by now I guess you could say "professor") of goal setting, I can say with 100 percent certainty that *Gratitude and Goals* demonstrates the right attitude and illustrates the right way to *create the life you would love to live!*

Paul J. Meyer

Founder of Success Motivation International, Inc.,
and 40 plus other companies and
New York Times best-selling author

PREFACE

From Dark Clouds To Bright Skies
How *Gratitude And Goals* Came To Be

"Success is not measured by what you accomplish but by the
opposition you have encountered, and the courage with which you
have maintained the struggle against overwhelming odds."

—ORISON SWETT MARDEN—

I want to tell you how this book came to be. In order to do
so, I need to tell you a bit about myself; about where I came
from and how I ended up where I am today. But before I begin, I
should make this brief disclaimer:

This is not a religious book. I am not promoting any particular
denomination, sect, or institution. It does not matter what your
religious beliefs are. But I want you to know that in order to fully
appreciate what is written in the following pages and gain the most
from what this book has to offer, you will need to have a spiritually
open mind. In other words, you must be willing to accept that
there is something (or *someone*) out there—a Higher Power of some
sort—that is greater than you. For the sake of simplicity, I have
chosen to refer to this something or someone as God.

Again, without any intention to offend or promote, I most
often use the pronouns Him, He or His when referring to God.
This does not mean that I necessarily embrace the view of a big
bearded guy sitting on a throne of clouds. It's just my preference. I

am not suggesting you adopt my view of a Higher Power, but I am asking you to be receptive to your own. So, if you find my choice of references distracting in any way, please feel free to replace them with your own (e.g., It, She/Her, Jesus, the Universe, Divine Intelligence, Great Spirit, Guru, Good-Orderly-Direction, Inner-self, Higher Consciousness, and so on).

Now, let's move on to the good stuff, shall we? This is where I get up close and personal, and tell you all about myself. I think if someone in Hollywood were to make a movie of my life so far (I know that's a little far-fetched, but anything's possible, right?), this is what it would look like . . .

Act One

Like many (maybe even *most*) others, I was born into a very dysfunctional family. At an early age I became a latchkey kid who learned to rely solely on myself. Because I never really felt like I fit in, I was a loner who preferred playing with my toys rather than with other kids my age.

As I got older, relationships were especially tough. I lived in constant fear that the person I was dating would one day "wake up" and realize I was no good, and then leave me for someone better. My neurotic thoughts and low self-esteem started to get the best of me. Although I desperately wanted the disparaging chatter in my head to stop, I just didn't seem to have the power to control it. With nowhere else to turn, I called my father and explained how I was feeling. He advised me, *"Every time those feelings come up, I want you to ask God to remove them."*

Desperate to change, but unfamiliar with the whole God thing, I relinquished my fears and did as he suggested. Whenever I felt the urge to go to that dark place in my head, I silently repeated, over and over, *"God, please remove these feelings."* Three weeks passed, and then suddenly one day, I realized that the horrible beliefs and emotions which had tormented me were gone. I was free! Today I can honestly say that, thanks to the God of my understanding, I'm no longer an overly insecure person.

Act Two

A couple years later, in 1997, my life seemed to be going well. I had a great job and was deeply in love. Time for some serious sabotaging! Always a weekend party girl, I started to drink heavily during the week as well. Anxiety and panic set in, along with the occasional bout of depression. I was no longer a fun, social drinker. Instead, I had become a complete Jekyll and Hyde. Some nights I was the life of the party; on others I got out of control, angry, even violent. I no longer enjoyed drinking, but didn't have the desire or the willpower to quit. The bottle and I developed a co-dependent relationship with one another; I needed it and it controlled me.

I consulted my doctor about the anxiety and panic attacks. She tried to help me with psychological treatments, stress management classes, and prescription drugs, but none of them worked. Things started to get bad: *really* bad. After one particularly regrettable night, I just couldn't take the pain anymore. I'd had enough. Broken and deflated, I suddenly dropped to my knees and began to cry—deep, aching sobs of despair. "*God, please help me. Please help me,*" I begged.

And then I heard a trusted voice, as clear as anything I had ever heard. It said to me, "*It's going to be okay. You're going to quit drinking and it's going to be okay.*"

It was God saving me again from the wreckage. And in that moment, all the anxiety, panic and depression disappeared, along with my obsession with alcohol. I felt completely protected; guided by something more powerful than myself. In that brief, unexpected moment, I got my life back and was saved from the hell that would surely have come. That day, God gave me a gift far greater than my sobriety. He gave me hope and faith—*in Him.* A few days later, I joined a spiritually based program of recovery and have been clean, sober and spiritual ever since.

I wish I could tell you that since that day my life has been joyous, happy, and free. But that isn't the way life works, is it?

Act Three

In 2006, my life was turned upside-down once more. My husband lost his business, the bank foreclosed on our home, and the government was demanding an insane amount of back taxes. We were in debt up to our eyeballs and at times there was barely enough money to buy groceries. Needless to say, I was financially, emotionally and spiritually bankrupt!

As the unopened bills piled up, I remained an unemployed, stay-at-home mother of two. To tell the truth, I couldn't have gone to work even if I'd wanted to. The cost of putting our two young children into daycare was more than I would have earned at any new job. I felt as though I had lost control over my life as it continued its downward spiral. So there I was, in my mid-thirties: I felt cheated and powerless, and yet guilty, too, because I was unable to help out financially. I fell into a cycle of self-pity, resentment and blame. I was angry with my husband because *he* had ruined my life. I was resentful of my children because *they* were holding me back. I blamed my mother because *she* had been an inadequate example. Although I felt justified, my constant nagging and complaining only made things worse.

And then I received another message from God. This time it came in the form of a DVD entitled *The Secret*. Its message was one I had heard before but had never been ready to receive. This is what *I heard* (not necessarily the exact words that were spoken) . . .

> *YOU are in control of your destiny. You must change your way of thinking and behaving if you want to change your life for the better. Positive thought reaps positive reward. No one can save you. You have to save yourself. Gratitude is the key!*

I suddenly knew, with complete inner clarity, that if what I wanted was a better life it was up to me to create it. I made a conscious decision to stop the blame game, right then and there; no more resentment, no more complaining, no more pity parties and no more negativity. I began to rethink our family's circumstances, taking responsibility for my part in the way things turned out. Instead of dwelling on the pain caused by past experiences, I refocused my energy on the positive. I started to love more and hate less. Lo and behold, my life unexpectedly began to blossom in so many beautiful ways.

I revitalized my marriage in a way that I would never have thought possible. I accepted my husband for who he was—a supportive person who had made mistakes just as I had. I recognized that the struggle I was having with my children stemmed from my own resentment, not from them. I realized how fortunate I was to be at home to watch them grow up. I became thankful for the lessons my mother had taught me. For the first time I truly understood that I was *not* my husband, my kids, my father, my mother, or my past. I was only me, and if I wanted a spectacular life, it was up to me to create it.

I began to practice gratitude throughout my day. By this simple shift in thinking—from an attitude of self-pity to one of abundance—I instantly became the master of my destiny. Gratitude gave me the confidence to want to do more, to be more and to have more. I was able to see that God had much bigger plans for me. I acknowledged my God-given talents and truly believed that, with Him by my side, I could do anything I set my mind to. This conviction soon became a burning desire to share with the world the principles which had not only changed my life but the lives of countless others. So, without delay, I set out to develop a daily gratitude journal to help others achieve the same positive shift I had achieved.

I had never been the type to follow through with distant plans. Always a great starter, I would typically lose focus a few days, weeks, or months into any new project, and quit. This time I was determined things would be different. I knew that if I wanted to succeed, I would have to develop some sort of goal setting system to overcome my usual hurdles (procrastination, laziness, and fear, to name a few), if I wanted to get the journal done. Based on my experience in the corporate world, I knew that goal setting worked, even though it never had for me. I had found that most goal setting methods focused too much attention on timelines and deadlines and not enough on *how* to achieve them. So I decided to give it another try—*my way*.

I came up with a simple, take-action goal setting program; one so easy to use that even a child (or a serial quitter like me) could be successful. Day-by-day, by steadily working at my goals, I conquered setbacks and insecurities that arose. No longer was I someone who just talked about what they wanted to do one day. I became someone who was actually doing it all—and loving every minute! My desire to develop a gratitude journal turned into a passion to offer people something so powerful that it would not only *inspire* them to want more from life, but it would actually guarantee that they *achieve* it, by giving them a place to steadily work at their goals every single day. And so, after many months of writing and research, the *Gratitude and Goals* Daily Journal was born.

Ever since this incredible journey began, my outer, "physical" world has continued to grow more exciting by the day. But the most fulfilling aspect has been on the inside. The things I have learned and continue to discover, such as faith, acceptance, self-compassion, autonomy and, of course, gratitude, are the tools I use to live my life now. Thanks to these principles, today I look only to myself to define who I am. I make my own mistakes and my own decisions, and I create my own successes. And the negative feelings which once controlled me have been replaced by confidence, love and inner peace.

One word of advice before we dig into the rest of the book: there's a line in *A Course in Miracles;* "Infinite patience produces immediate results," which presents one of those wonderful para-doxes of spiritual growth. If you approach this program with the attitude that you're in it for the long haul, your life will begin to change immediately. On the other hand, if you grab onto it looking for a quick fix, you'll be disappointed.

I am *thrilled* that you've chosen to go on this journey with me. It's never too late to change the course of your life. Stop wasting *your* precious time. Seize the day. Life is too short not to!

My deepest gratitude today and always,

Stacey Grewal

ACKNOWLEDGMENTS

Thursday, November 26, 2009
(Thanksgiving Day)

It may be ironic or simply a matter of fate that today of all days, Thanksgiving Day, I am writing this note of thanks to the many who have helped me along the way in writing this book.

First, thank you, God, for giving me the opportunity to take this wonderful and wondrous journey. Thank you for being by my side and seeing me through the good times and the bad. For all that I am and all that I have, thank you. I have no complaints.

The next thank you is certainly special. To my two beautiful children, Jagger and Kash, I want you to know that I love you more than words can ever explain. Jagger, you were three years old and Kash, you were only one when I started writing this book. Now you are six and three, respectively. Thank you for allowing me to use our experiences together as material for my book. You have both been such an inspiration to me. And thank you for being so patient with me when I was too "busy working" to spend time with you. I so appreciate how amazingly understanding you both were.

To Ruby, my ever-supportive husband and confidant, I owe immeasurable gratitude. Even though times got tough financially, it was you who realized that pursuing my dreams was more important than my putting time and energy into a job that I would hate. You always believed in me and this project; you respected the time and labor that I had to put into it. Thank you! We've had hard times that motivated us to think big. Let's never forget them; those memories will enable us to enjoy the good times even more. And I would be remiss if, at this time, I didn't thank Ruby's entire family for graciously being my caring extended family. Thank you for your unconditional love and support.

Thank you, Mom, for helping me to realize what it takes to become the woman that I want to be. And, Dad, thank you for always listening to me and encouraging every one of my endeavors. You lent me your vision of God when I could not see one of my own and you planted the seeds of faith in me when I had nothing to sow.

To my big brother, Terry, whose back and forth banter I cherish. In many ways, we are soul mates on this precious earth. We understand one another instinctively. I believe in you. Thank you for constantly believing in me.

I offer a special thanks to my beautiful grandmother, Aline. You are ninety-five and you still possess an incredible thirst for life and a desire for personal growth. You took me under your loving wing when I was young. You have my sincerest gratitude. Although I don't call you often, you are in my mind and heart every day.

To Uncle Mike for giving our family *The Secret* when times were ever so tough, thank you. If it weren't for that gift, I truly believe I would not have written this book. Also, I have to thank the rest of my family (and you know who you are) for your continuous words of encouragement and faith.

At times, I am a big dreamer who just wants to be heard. To the so many friends too innumerable to list here, thank you for patiently listening to me. I want to give a special thanks to my best friend, Barbra. At times you were confident in me and my abilities when I felt I had none. Thank you for always listening to me and for encouraging every single creative idea I've ever had.

And there are so many who have taken the time to help me package this, my first book. Thank you to Andy, Keith, Debbie, Melissa, Ken, Lindsay, David, Paul and Dr. Jay. You have all in some way helped lift me to "pro" status. I would also like to make a note of gratitude to some very "special" friends who went out of their way to help me make this book so it's more than just another dust collector: Marina Degteva, Brian Mast, Maria Morgis and Domo Kovacevic.

Finally, I offer a special "thank you" to Paul J. Meyer, who passed away on October 27, 2009, just one month after writing the *foreword* for this book. Mr. Meyer, you are a leader of great distinction! Thank you, for believing that my message can help others achieve the life of their dreams, just as yours has helped so many others. I am very grateful for the time and effort you put into writing such a wonderful *foreword* for me, especially since you were going through a difficult time with your illness. And although you do not know it, you, your words and your courage, have been, and always will be one of my greatest mentors.

As I mentioned, as I write this, it is the official day that we in America give thanks. Let's remember that gratitude is more than giving thanks once a year. It's important to give thanks every day. What are you waiting for? Tell someone, "thank you" today.

And finally, to you, my cherished readers . . . "Thank you!"

INTRODUCTION

"Each morning we are born again.
What we do today is what matters most."

—BUDDHA—

Tick tock. Tick tock. Can you hear it? It's the sound of life passing you by . . .

You've heard that fateful ticking, haven't you? Maybe it caught your attention at 3 a.m. when you were lying in bed, tossing and turning, unable to sleep. Maybe you heard it when your feet hit the floor on a Monday morning and your heart said, "Not another week of *this.*" You know that the amazing life you've always dreamed of is inside you just waiting to be born. You can feel it. And yet, somehow, today doesn't seem like the day it will happen. Maybe tomorrow. Maybe next month. Maybe next year. And so the clock keeps ticking. *Tick tock. Tick tock.*

It doesn't have to be that way!

You have exactly 86,400 chances to change your life each and every day. That's right. Every second of every day is a new moment.

Snap your fingers. See; new moment! Oh, there's another one! And another! Each new moment literally holds *infinite* power within it. And with every breath you take, you're given another opportunity to either play it safe or to do something spectacular. It doesn't matter what choices you've made in the millions of moments leading up to this one. In THIS moment you have the power to choose differently.

This is *your* moment. How do you want to live it?

Gratitude and Goals is a two part book (Book One and Book Two). It is a step-by-step, instructional guide *and* a daily gratitude, goal setting and personal growth journal, written for the millions who have settled for a mundane life, a mediocre job and ho-hum relationships; but who know they want and deserve more. More happiness, deeper love, greater wealth, better health, heightened spirituality, explosive success and inner peace. It's for those who want to be the very best they can be and who want to experience all they've ever dreamed of. It's for those who want to feel the throb of passion and purpose in every waking moment, but who have been either too busy or too afraid, or who just haven't known *how* to achieve it.

❦

Knowing how to utilize the incredible powers of gratitude is the key to success and fulfillment in all areas of your life.

❦

What if you could wake up tomorrow morning, and every morning thereafter, excited about your life? And by excited, I don't just mean happy to be alive; I mean *really* looking forward to each day. Imagine opening your eyes and having your very first thought be, "Thank you, God, for this wonderful day and all the opportunity it holds." I do this every single day. It's what I call "gratitude."

While everyone knows what it means to say "thank you," few realize the staggering benefits of a life filled with gratitude. I'm not just talking about being thankful for the things you "should" be grateful for, such as the roof over your head and the food on your plate. Of course it's important to be thankful for those things. But what you may not realize is that gratitude's potential goes far beyond an appreciation for what you have. It is a way of living that can completely alter the way you look at your past, change your present behavior and profoundly impact your future.

In my experience, most people who lecture on the subject of gratitude merely skim the surface when describing this powerful force. This book digs deeper; connecting faith with fortune and gratitude with goal setting.

Gratitude and Goals is for those who have waded through piles of "inspirational" books that promise, "You can have everything!" but who still find themselves eating the boxed macaroni and cheese dinner of life. I don't know about you, but I've found many of the popular "self-help" books to be long on promise, but short on delivery. They fail to create any real, lasting results. Well, I'm happy to tell you that *this book is different.*

⊱⋅⊰

Grateful people are happy, confident people who are likely to actively set and achieve new goals.

⊱⋅⊰

Book One, titled, *You Are the Master of Your Today and the Creator of Your Tomorrow* is a "how to" manual, spiritual teacher, personal coach and mentor. It is filled with valuable gratitude and goal setting strategies, easy to follow instructions, examples, experience and quick exercises to help you achieve the physical, emotional and spiritual prosperity you desire. It thoroughly explains *why* gratitude works, *what* you can do to achieve this remarkable feeling, and most importantly, *how* you can use this skill to confidently set and achieve new long term, short term and daily goals.

Study after study shows that goal setting works! Goal setting has been proven to be the best way of translating your visions and hopes into reality, by putting the reins of result-oriented action in your hands. But goal setting is not a one-shot deal. It is a *process*. This book will teach you the day-to-day, fail-proof goal setting process that can turn any quitter into a conqueror, the very first time they try it.

The daily practice of gratitude, combined with goal setting, is like a perfect marriage. They motivate, drive, and influence each other *harmoniously*. Gratitude creates confidence, inspiring you to want more, and goal setting helps you achieve it! With each goal met, you will be looking to achieve a bigger and better goal, and then another, and so forth. And with each success, you will be given another reason to deepen your gratitude. It's cyclical. You will also learn why so many people fail to complete their goals, and how *you* can avoid these pitfalls!

At the end of the day, it doesn't really matter how much money or success you have in the material world if you're not completely satisfied with the emotional, intellectual and spiritual progress you're making on the inside. If what you want is a better life—to *have* more, *do* more, and *be* more, and to freely delight in your success when it does come—you need to start then, by improving yourself from the inside-out.

Gratitude and Goals is a complete mind, body, and spirit system, designed to help you increase self-awareness and serenity. It will help you identify those things which are running counter to your dreams, then motivate you to become accountable, and *committed* to changing them. After only a few weeks of working this program, you will be astonished to find that not only has your overall success rate increased, but you will be on a new path towards enlightenment.

The *Gratitude and Goals* Daily Journal is a tireless plan of action. Research has proven that people who keep a daily, personal development journal experience an immeasurable increase in happiness, hope, love, health, enthusiasm and success. They exercise more regularly, and are also generally more optimistic about each day and the direction of their life as a whole.

Book Two: the *Gratitude and Goals* Daily Journal, is a practical, hands-on application for those who want to do more than just talk (or *read*) about changing. It is a gratitude list, a goal setting journal, a personal growth support system, a to-do list, a memo pad and a progress tracker, with sixty daily journal-style, fill-in-the-blank pages that you just won't find in any other book. And it is so easy to use that you are guaranteed to experience real results *the very first time you use it.*

The *Gratitude and Goals* Daily Journal is about creating solutions—not stewing in problems. It's about taking action, not making excuses. By understanding, and more importantly, *working through* this simple program, you will have all the tools you need to build the life you dream of and deserve. But it's not enough to simply read this book. It can't do the work for you. YOU must be willing to take committed action in order to make it happen.

In just ten to fifteen minutes each day, the *Gratitude and Goals* Daily Journal will forever change the way you live your life. You will accomplish more in the first thirty days of using it than you ever did before you had a plan of action. It will help you turn any hobby into a career, start a business, earn a degree, find true love, lose twenty (*or even* 120) pounds, clean the garage, improve your golf game, learn how to play an instrument, read *War and Peace*, or maybe write a book of your own. It can even completely alter your way of life, helping you become a better, more successful and happier person, in all areas of your life.

There is little room for negativity in a life ignited by the light of gratitude and focused by the power of goals. By reading this book and working through the *Gratitude and Goals* Daily Journal, you will be empowered to take control of your life. You will begin to think, feel, and behave more in tune with your dreams. You will come to know your Higher Power and have faith in a partnership with Him. Your outlook will change, your awareness will increase, and you will gain the strength to push away any external blocks standing in the way of your success. All the self-defeating beliefs which have held you back will be replaced with a new, positive attitude and an enthusiasm for life. Not only will you start to see opportunities, you will begin to *create* them.

No matter who you are or where you come from, regardless of your age, race, education, social status, or upbringing, you can live the most incredible life imaginable—*the one you would love to live!* The very fact that you can dream it means it's meant to be. And the fact that you bought this book means you are *ready* to realize your full potential.

I intentionally made this book short and sweet. Everything you need to create the life of your dreams is already locked inside of you (even if you don't realize it). *Gratitude and Goals* is the key to making it happen. Now all you have to do is take action!

This is *your* life. What are you waiting for?

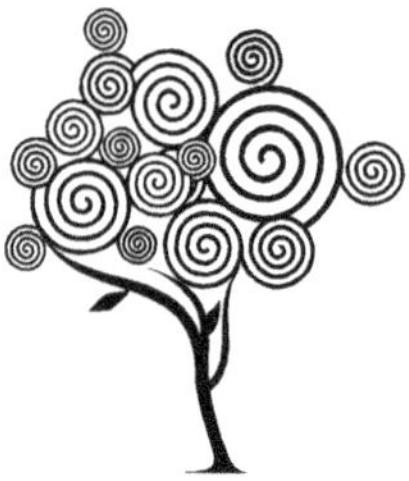

BOOK ONE

You Are the Master of Your Today and the Creator of Your Tomorrow

Chapter One

IT IS YOUR GOD-GIVEN RIGHT TO HAVE IT ALL

"... the kingdom of God is within you."

—LUKE 17:21—

 H ow do you know if you're meant to be rich? Well, do you want nice things? If you answered, "yes," then you were *meant* to be rich. The same goes for love, health, happiness, success, or just about anything else you desire. If you can dream it, God intended you to have it.

God *wants* you to be happy. He wants you to be in love. He wants you to have nice things. He wants you to be wealthy; *really wealthy*. Not just in dollars, but in everything this garden of Earth offers. God did not put us here so we can struggle. It isn't His master plan to torture us by planting burning desires in our hearts and then keeping us from achieving them. Why else would He have given you so many amazing talents and such vivid dreams if He didn't want you to use them to your advantage?

As a child of God, it's your God-given right to have it all ...

You have a right to be rich.

You have a right to hold out for true love.

3

You have a right to work at your dream job.

You have a right to the best education possible.

You have a right to own nice things.

You have a right to be healthy.

You have a right to wholesome, nutritious food.

You have a right to marry whomever you want.

You have a right to be single if you want to be.

You have a right to travel and meet new people.

You have a right to be happy!

Many people, especially those who are of particular beliefs, believe we should live with less than we desire, out of humility. They criticize those who want more out of life. Humility does not mean going without. It's simply acknowledging that our gifts come from a higher place. Failing to maximize such gifts is not heroic; it's merely an insult to the Giver.

Let me ask you, which man's efforts do you think the world would benefit from most; a poor man who devotes his life to helping the few less-than-fortunate of his community, or a wealthy man who spends millions of his hard earned dollars helping thousands of people across the globe? Do you think God loves one more than the other? It really doesn't matter who creates the most effective campaign. God loves them both, equally, as He does us all. And, if they have equally good intentions, both should be applauded for their efforts.

We all want more. More money. More love. More friends. More knowledge. More health. More excitement. More time.

More inner peace. More spirituality. More to have and more to give. *More everything!* And that's okay. In fact, it's better than okay; it's completely natural. And it's exactly the way God created us. The world needs you to be wealthy *in all areas of your life.* When we strive to be the best we can be, everyone benefits from our success. When we stop wanting more, we stop contributing to mankind. And it's when we stop advancing in life that we begin to die.

No matter what others would have us think, we are all worthy of—*and are entitled to*—the same opportunities. God didn't create racism, sexism, the class system, religion, or any other means of separating His children. Humanity created these forms of oppression as a way to keep others down. The fact is that there are rich, successful, fulfilled people from all walks of life, from all neighborhoods, and from all gene pools; *including yours.*

Choice, *Not* Chance, Determines Your Destiny

Life is not controlled by fate, history, DNA, habit, or predetermined destiny, but by choice. You get to choose how your life will unfold from this moment on. You can choose to be the driver or the passenger; the puppeteer or the puppet. You can choose to be happy or fulfilled. Even your thoughts are within your control. You can choose either to be a victim of them or to *use* them as a springboard to something great.

Deep down, everyone wants to be the best, to do the most they can, to fulfill their dreams, and to leave behind a legacy. But if you are living less than the life you desire, you should know that you are holding you back. No one else is doing it to you. The only thing you're limited by is your own thinking. Life is meant to be abundant; really abundant *for everyone*. If you have the perception that you are *less deserving* than anyone else in this world, *you* are stalling your own advancement.

"But by the grace of God I am what I am: and his grace which was bestowed upon me was not in vain; but I labored more abundantly than they all: yet not I, but the grace of God which was with me."

—1 CORINTHIANS 15:10—

I was already two years into writing this book when I was hit with fear that all my work was just a big waste of time. Although part of me was confident in the future *Gratitude and Goals* was creating for me, and of course I was very grateful for it, yet some insecurity and doubt remained that I was unworthy of the kind of success I dreamed of.

Although I was taking the right kind of action, my lack of self confidence kept me from believing it could really happen for me. I was fearful that no one would read my book because I didn't have an M.D or Ph.D. behind my name, or the kind of recognition the Jack Canfield's or Tony Robbins' of the world had. Not to mention the fact that no one in my inner circle had ever achieved the kind of success I desired. Who was I to think I could break free from the bondage of my self-defeatist attitude and succeed?

I knew I had to change my beliefs and get over this hurdle if I were to receive my just rewards. And then it hit me. As Dr. Maxwell Maltz states in his book, *The New Psycho-Cybernetics*, "holding a low opinion of ourselves is not a virtue, but a vice. Stop carrying around a mental picture of yourself as a person less capable than others, by making unfair apples-to-oranges comparisons. Celebrate your victories small or large, recognize and build on your strengths, and continually remind yourself that you are not your mistakes."

I've since come to understand; we will always be compensated for the value of the services we provide. In other words, we'll be compensated according to what people are *willing* to pay for our services. You might be saying, "What about the teacher who works her butt off and gets paid less than her worth? And what about the actors in Hollywood who get millions for child's play? Why are they getting paid so much? It just doesn't seem fair." It may not seem fair, but the fact remains; something is only worth what other people are willing to pay for it. Unfortunately, most people would rather pay more to be entertained than to be educated!

I came up with this mantra to remove my self-doubt and shift my way of thinking: "I deserve *everything* I am working towards." This simple affirmation changed my mindset. I began to give myself credit for the perseverance and hard work that I was continuously and faithfully putting in. No longer did I see myself as someone who was undeserving. I recognized that I was simply looking to be compensated for my efforts.

Marianne Williamson's poem *"Our Deepest Fear"* beautifully sums up what I'm getting at:

"Our deepest fear is not that we are inadequate. Our deepest fear is that we are powerful beyond measure. It is our light, not our darkness that most frightens us. We ask ourselves, who am I to be brilliant, gorgeous, talented, fabulous? Actually, who are you not to be? You are a child of God. Your playing small does not serve the world. There's nothing enlightened about shrinking so that other people won't feel insecure around you. We are all meant to shine, as children do. We were born to make manifest the glory of God that is within us. It's not just in some of us; it's in everyone. And as we let our own light shine, we unconsciously give other people permission to do the same. As we're liberated from our own fear, our presence automatically liberates others."

Eight hours a day is eight hours a day no matter how you spend it. Some people spend that time flipping burgers for minimum wage because they think that's all they are worth, while others make thousands of dollars in that same time doing what they love. There is really no difference between them. They both work towards what they feel they are worth and *they both get paid accordingly*. You might be saying, "What if the one has a Harvard MBA while the other is a high school dropout?" I agree. It is more difficult to make money if you are seriously disadvantaged, but, as the saying goes, where there is a will there is a way. The question is: *what is your will?*

Most of us, if given the chance to have millions of dollars, a flawless life partner, or a thriving business at the push of a button, would gleefully push the button. But that's nothing more than wishful thinking. Success, in all areas of your life, requires work. Those who seem to have it all get what they deserve by meeting their destiny, not by waiting for it to fall into their laps. They *will* their way to success.

Robert Kiyosaki, author of *Rich Dad, Poor Dad*, says, "Many people fail to become rich because they value a steady paycheck rather than going through the learning process of becoming financially smarter." There are many ways to become a huge success without a diploma or family connections, but you must be willing to have faith that you deserve it, and take the appropriate actions to make it happen. If you want something badly enough to go after it, it means you're destined to have it (providing you don't hurt another to get it, of course). Notice, however, that I said, "if you want something *badly enough to go after it.*" That hunger inside is God's way of telling you: "Go for it. You CAN do this."

Thoughts, *Not* People, Rule the World

It's no longer a matter of debate; thought creates and controls everything, even reality. Thought creates feelings of hate and it also creates love. It creates resentment and it can also create forgiveness. No war has ever been waged, nor has any kindness ever been offered, without a thought behind it. Thought creates molecules in our bodies that are either helpful or harmful. Thoughts, *or more importantly,* our perception of them, can create feelings of happiness and wellbeing; they can also create *dis*-ease.

What your life is like on the outside is merely a reflection of what you think and feel on the inside. Take a moment and think about how you interact with the world. Do you go through life happy, joyous and free? Or are you often frustrated; complaining about one thing or another? If you tend to foster a negative state inside, you will see your life and the world around you as unfair and cruel. If you're generally positive and upbeat, you will see the world around you as being filled with endless possibilities and love.

Norman Vincent Peale, author of *The Power of Positive Thinking*, says you can, "Change your thoughts, and you change your world." Your thoughts can literally attract people, things, and events into your life that are of similar frequencies; "like attracts like." If your mind focuses on the negative aspects of your life, it will continue to create and attract more negative results. When your mind focuses on the positive, it will create and attract more of the same. You are the sovereign ruler of everything that happens between your ears. Only you get to choose what you are thinking.

Our thoughts and feelings go hand in hand. Thoughts are what *give rise* to our feelings. They also alter how we *interpret* them. When you think about debts that need paying, you feel one way. When you think about your loving dog, you feel another. If you want to change your feelings, you need to first change your thoughts about them. Positive thoughts produce positive feelings, which produce positive outcomes. Our inner state changes first, then our outer state follows.

In order to make better sense of this, I've separated feelings into two categories:

1. **Our purest feelings.**

   Also known as our "gut" feelings or instincts. They are a reflection of our truest intentions. Awareness of these feelings is the key to our enlightenment.

2. **The feelings we choose to experience.**

   These are our most accessible feelings. They are the ones we most often express and which are most easily influenced by our thoughts. They are also the ones which most often inspire us to make "rash" decisions.

Most of us don't realize the power our feelings have. If we listen closely to our purest feelings, they will tell us what is right and what is wrong (for us, and for life in general). It is often too difficult to access them, though. They can become so muddled by our thoughts that the two (thoughts and feelings) are often confused for one another. We don't *use* our feelings proactively, but reactively; *passively rather than actively.* That is, we look at what's going on in our lives and adjust our feelings according to what we see. If our spouse speaks hurtfully to us or an unexpected bill comes due, dread sets in and we "have a bad day." We tell ourselves this is an appropriate reaction.

Our feelings are thermostats rather than thermometers. That is, we can change the quality of our lives by *deliberately choosing* to feel better, not by passively taking on the emotional "temperature" of those around us. Just as one raises the temperature in a room by setting the thermostat higher, we can change our lives by raising our inner emotional temperature. We do this by choosing thoughts and actions which lead to "higher frequency" feelings.

Try a simple experiment. Walk into a shop, office, or restaurant with an inner attitude of total, unconditional love for everyone you meet in there. Put a smile on your face and maintain an inner feeling of love. Notice how people respond to you differently. Notice the attraction you hold. Notice how good *you* feel!

If you wanted to, you could deliberately choose to feel bad right now too. All you'd have to do is focus your thoughts on something or someone who has done you harm. If you think about it strongly enough, allowing yourself to feel the emotions of that time they hurt you, you will begin to experience the pain all over again. You can even think about something that hasn't happened yet, and it can change the way you feel. If you let it, it can even make you sick to your stomach.

When was the last time you had to make a presentation or a speech in front of a room full of people? How did you feel in the minutes, days, or even *weeks* leading up to that moment? The number one fear most people have is a fear of public speaking. It even ranks above dying, if you can believe it. And yet, the most stressful part of any public speaking engagement is not the actual moment when the words start coming out of your mouth, but the many moments leading up to that one; when you *think* about having to do it. On the flip side, the anticipation of a big vacation can sometimes turn out to be more exciting than the trip itself.

It's been said that life is ten percent what happens to us and ninety percent how we react to what happens to us. We may not be able to control an outcome, but we can give it new meaning simply by changing our thoughts about it. How else can something like a speech or bankruptcy become a death sentence for one person and a catapult to a better life for another, if not for a difference of perception?

No matter what you believe, the fact remains that you (and your perceptions) are completely responsible for your life and the way it has turned out. All the thoughts, feelings and decisions you've made up until this point have been your own. No one is to blame for what you do or don't have, where you are in life, or what you may or may not have become. Yes, others have influenced you in some way; but your thoughts, your choices, and the actions and reactions that have flowed from them are, and always have been, completely within your control.

Most of us hate to hear that we are responsible for the negative aspects of our lives. We quickly try to point out how some other person or situation is really to blame. But the glorious part of being responsible for everything that happens to you is that you, *and only you*, have the power to rewrite your life as you want it to be . . .

No one can make you think, feel or do anything you don't want to.

No one can make you rich and no one can keep you poor; if you don't want to be.

No one can make you stay at a job or in a relationship you don't want to be in. And no one can make you run the other way.

No one can make you enjoy something you don't want to enjoy.

No one can make you feel something you don't want to feel.

No one can keep you from creating goals and going after them. And no one can make you follow through.

So . . . what do you want to have? What do you want to achieve? Who do you want to be? It is completely up to you.

"We were born to succeed, not fail."

—HENRY DAVID THOREAU—

We're all products of our upbringings. But that doesn't mean we have to be victims of them. Past hurts and experiences are yesterday's news. They do not determine who you are or who you're going to be. They are the tire tracks behind the car of your life, not the engine driving it.

Your only limitations are your present thoughts, and the feelings they produce. Weakening, depressing thoughts hold no value. In fact, they are actively harming you. If you believe you are disadvantaged in any way, you will cause that belief to manifest in your outer world. Only by removing false thoughts of limitation can you be all that you are capable of being. This is truly the mechanism by which your life will change.

Today, you have a chance to cast a new vote by *deliberately choosing* the thoughts you think. Start by thinking positively. Positive thinking is not about pretending that your problems don't exist. It's about acknowledging your problems, and then changing your perception of them, so that you can come up with solutions to resolve them. The moment fear, doubt, or judgment set in; stop them dead in their tracks. Choose a more positive, proactive thought; or simply be grateful for whatever opportunity your problem presents.

Reclaim your life by exercising deliberate control over your thoughts. Don't listen to the negative voices in your head. When you hear one telling you that you're not capable or worthy, tell it to take a hike! You're in charge of your thoughts now. The more you exercise that authority, the better you will get at it. You deserve to have the life you dream of, but it is up to you to create it. Everything that has happened before this moment is a "was" or an "up until now." The only moment that *counts* is NOW. Every breath is a new moment; a chance to start rewriting the script of your life and begin using the gifts God gave you.

Now let's talk about HOW you will accomplish this . . .

Chapter Two

THE POWER OF
PURPOSEFUL PRAYER

"People who can sincerely be thankful for the things which they own only in imagination have real faith. They will get rich; they will cause the creation of whatever they want."

—WALLACE WATTLES—

D o you pray? If you answered "yes" then I have one question for you; *Why?* Why do you pray? Many people pray, but far fewer know *why* they do so (or even *how to*). Some pray because they were taught to when they were young. Others believe it's their only way into heaven. Some do it out of a sense of duty or fear. Many pray to improve their conscious contact with their Higher Power, while others don't even know *why* they pray; they just do it out of habit or cultural expectation.

The power of prayer is truly awesome when done with *purpose*. Purposeful prayer is so influential that it can completely trans-form your life; creating renewed optimism, faith, and hope. It can pick you up when you're down and give you strength when times are tough. Purposeful prayer will grant you clarity when you're confused and give you courage when you're scared. It will increase stamina so that you keep pushing forward and bestow on you a newfound stillness and inner peace you may never have known.

What *Is* Purposeful Prayer?

The answer to this question is quite simple, yet too often becomes complicated and confusing; thanks to the many different myths and belief systems. Purposeful prayer is concentrated, *meaningful* conversation with your Higher Power. A purposeful prayer doesn't need to be said in a certain way, with a certain verse or words. Nor does it need to be done at a particular time of day or in a particular setting. You don't have to be on your knees or in a church to pray. It's not only for those who claim they're the chosen few or who think it will save them from a burning hell. Prayer is for everyone, at any time, in any way.

Prayers aren't necessarily those things which you memorize and repeat, like the prayers you were taught as a child. Those do not always carry a lot of power. I grew up with the belief that the best way to pray to God was by reciting the *Lord's Prayer*. I mean, it is called the *Lord's Prayer*, so it must be endorsed by the powers that be, right? I never actually listened to, or cared about the words, but that didn't matter. As long as it was the *Lord's Prayer* I was reciting, I felt I must have been praying the right way.

For many years I prayed in this ritualistic way, even though it failed to raise my spirits or make me feel connected. It just seemed to be a formal exercise; something I did mainly out of fear (of being a sinner, going to hell, you name it). One thing I know now is that the *Lord's Prayer*, or any other prayer, is completely meaningless unless it's said *with meaning*.

Each denomination and/or faith has its own book of prayer. When it comes to choosing the right prayer for you it doesn't matter which book or what religion it comes from. The magic is not in the words themselves, but in your *belief* in the words. Whether or not it works for you is not determined by how perfect the prayer is but by the amount of faith you have when saying it.

Gratitude taught me how to pray. It showed me that it was more important to *thank* God for what He had already given me, instead of asking for more. I stopped asking God to tell me how I should be living my life; instead I thanked Him for His guidance and for always being there for me. I stopped believing that my talents were of no value; instead I thanked Him for my gifts and the amazing future I was creating with them. I thanked Him for guiding me every day, for helping me to be the best person, and parent I could be, and for giving me an opportunity to learn, and be better through my mistakes. The more thanks I gave, the more apparent those things became in my life.

When I became grateful, the time spent in prayer was no longer the monotonous, empty ritual of the past. It flourished into an amazing, meditative, open dialogue with my Higher Power. I began to honestly talk and listen to, the God of my understanding. I became conscious of a world filled with abundance and opportunity. Finally, I had the relationship with God that I had always yearned for. Whether I prayed for one minute or twenty, when I was done I felt lifted; filled with a renewed sense of love and faith that all the years of "ritual" prayer had never given me.

Gratitude is the way to the Creator. I believe that the reason so many people have such a hard time connecting with God is because they do not know how to be truly grateful. They read holy books and believe *that* is who or what God is—a bunch of written rules and regulations. They pray without knowing how to pray and without really understanding what they're going to gain from it (except to escape damnation). When you know how to live gratefully, you can begin to see God as more than this intimidating illusion, but as your all-loving and trusting partner in life. He gives you everything you need and it's through purposeful prayer that you become open to receiving it.

NOTE: Spirituality is subjective. Each person's spirituality is as unique and as special as their DNA and should be respected as such, regardless of how (by way of religion, suffering, mistakes, upbringing, etc.) they attain it. Whatever path you take to get to God is the right path for YOU. Don't let anyone tell you otherwise.

One day I came across the most amazing little prayer;

For all that I am and all that I have, I am grateful.
I have no complaints.

It may not seem awe-inspiring at first glance, but once you understand the message you will see why I love it so. It says that you HAVE within YOURSELF, the power to make whatever you want of your life—past, present, and future. You are without need of anything outside of yourself and God. You have no reason to complain, *ever*, as long as you believe this to be true!

I added it to my prayers before going to bed every night. I made sure that every time I said it, I did so with passion and belief. And then the most remarkable thing started to happen. My feelings of gratitude deepened and the difficulties I faced in my daily life became more manageable and less significant. I feared less and my confidence began to grow. My intuition soared and my self-awareness exploded . . . anger, guilt and shame slowly slipped away.

How to Pray, the Purposeful Way

Allow me to start by telling you one of the most important things you'll ever come to know. Anyone, yes, *anyone* can have a conversation with God. Not just priests, ministers, gurus, rabbis, or nuns, and not just someone who writes a book called *Conversations with God*; but *anyone*. Including you!

As I explained, any attempt at meaningful conversation with God is prayer. But if you're having trouble focusing, here's a simple solution: quiet your mind, concentrate your thoughts on the moment, and tell yourself you're talking to *someone* who is really listening. Think of Him as an intimate friend and mentor who wants nothing but the best for you. Think of Him as someone who does not judge you and who loves you unconditionally. In my opinion, that is the only definition of God. Keep your God-space as a place of pure and utter honesty. Talk to Him as someone you can trust, without reservation. Tell Him how you feel. Be true in your intentions, without the self-censorship, deceit, or lies.

For many, a close, personal relationship with God remains elusive. They go through life unsure about their purpose because they aren't connecting with or understanding God's will for them. It's not that they're failing to ask God about the meaning of their existence; it's that they're failing to ask the *right* kind of questions. Coming to know God and His will for you is not as hard as you may think.

I've always been taught, "When in doubt, ask God for guidance." I must have wasted half my life asking Him to give me things or do for things for me, with few or no results. Why? Well, my mistake was assuming that God was not already giving me everything I needed. Understanding the words, *all that I am and all that I have*, I've come to see that God already *does* for me what I can't do for myself. He guides me every day, throughout the day, without my even realizing it.

To ask God to help you is to assume that His help is not already given.

Confused? Here's an example. Let's say you were hungry but were lucky enough to own an endless bag of rice. However, you didn't know how to cook it. Would it make sense to ask God to send you more rice in order to vanquish your hunger? No. Wouldn't it make more sense to ask instead how to cook it? Well, your relationship with God is much the same. You work as one team. He's given and continues to give you everything you need; it's up to you to open your eyes to the possibilities, and to do the very best with what you have been given.

Instead of asking for more guidance, then, thank God for the guidance He already gives you. Ask God to remove all things blocking you from recognizing the wisdom and the awareness that is *already in you*, so that you can know His guidance. Don't just ask God to bless your family; give thanks that He *already has* and continues to do so every day. Pray to learn from your mistakes so that you can become a better person (parent, spouse, teacher, employer, friend, and so on).

Instead of asking for more, give thanks for what you have—because you already have everything you need. Pray to God to help you know the gifts He's given you and to show you how to use them. And if you're having trouble with any of this, ask for clarity and it will be given. God's timing is always perfect. He knows what you need, including when and how you need it, better than you do.

"God Helps Those Who Help Themselves"

There is a difference between depending on God to satisfy your every need and asking for His help. God can and will perform miracles, often doing for us what we can't do for ourselves. For example, there are millions of people worldwide who can say without a doubt that God saved them from the disease of alcoholism when there seemed to be no hope. I know of such miracles because I am one of them. But if you think it's His (or the world's) job to make sure you have a perfect life, without you having to do the work, then you will most likely live your days unfulfilled.

God is a gentleman. He won't force Himself upon you. If you don't ask for help, He will assume you don't want it. He will keep his distance, allowing you to make your own mistakes. It's not up to God to change our minds for us. That's something we have to do on our own. If you wish to know God's guidance, you need only to ask for it. When you're sincere in your intentions and your desire is backed by faith, *then* you will be capable of receiving His help, either by miracle or empowerment.

The other night, I was watching the movie *Evan Almighty*. It's a cute, modern day version of Noah's Ark, starring Steve Carell (Noah) and Morgan Freeman (God). One of the most powerful scenes in the movie occurs when Noah's upset and confused wife confides in God (disguised as a waiter) about her problems with her husband, who seems to have lost his mind. God responds, "*Let me ask you something; if someone prays for patience, do you think God gives them patience, or does He give them the opportunity to be patient? If he prayed for courage, does God give him courage, or does He give him opportunities to be courageous? If someone prayed for the family to be closer, do you think God zaps them with warm fuzzy feelings, or does He give them opportunities to love each other?*"

Nothing in life is a given, except change. Change can be terrifying, especially if it is forced upon you, such as a job loss or a sudden illness. But what seems bad today may actually be a blessing tomorrow. It's okay to grieve the passing of what once felt so safe and comfortable. But it's not okay to become the grief. See change as an opportunity for something better; not as the end of the world, but as the beginning of a new era. Change can be very exciting, if you use this time to focus on solutions rather than the problem. It forces us to make decisions about what we want for our future. *What are my dreams? What matters to me most? What do I want to be doing for the rest of my life?* Take time to reflect and research all possibilities.

God has infinite knowledge. He works according to what He knows is best for us, not necessarily in accordance with our humanly wishes. God may not give us what we ask for when we ask for it, but He does provide us with an opportunity to get it for ourselves. It's been said that God will never give you more than you can handle. That goes for both obstacles *and* blessings. The benefit you seek may not come when you want it, but when you're fully ready to receive it. I have found that often when I ask for blessings and have faith they will be given, what I end up realizing is that the blessings I asked for were right in front of my face the whole time.

God is our partner in life. When we speak to Him honestly and openly, and have faith in His powers, we become empowered to do anything we set our minds to. Pray for the ability to see, and then act on the messages with your newfound confidence. There will always be setbacks, but with God by your side we can and will get through them.

"As human beings, we are endowed with freedom of choice, and we cannot shuffle off our responsibility upon the shoulders of God or nature. We must shoulder it ourselves. It is up to us."

—ARNOLD J. TOYNBEE—

Not too long ago, a friend of mine named, Jenny, was going through a difficult time trying to have a baby. Miscarriage after painful miscarriage occurred and she couldn't understand why. Why the loss? Why the suffering? *Why her?* Although there were many medical reasons for her difficulties, Jenny continued to be disillusioned and confused. She was angry with God because He didn't answer her prayers. She didn't understand His plan for her, so she felt abandoned and betrayed. Jenny began to lose faith in her once all-powerful Higher Power.

I told Jenny I believed God *did* give her the answers she was looking for, but she simply wasn't listening. She didn't really want to know *why* she miscarried. Deep down, she knew why. She just wanted God to fix her so she could have a healthy baby. What she wanted was a miracle.

Millions of people all over the world suffer from one illness or another. They go to doctors looking to be healed. When they're not, they blame God. Humanity's problems—obesity, addiction, anxiety, and most of the other health and environmental issues we experience—are human-made, not God-made. They are created by the choices we collectively make.

Manufacturers use pesticides and other chemicals to make the things we want cheaper and quicker. Then, when we get sick from all the toxins, we turn to the pharmaceutical industry to cure us—these companies thrive on our poor health and have little intention of "curing" anything. We build homes on the banks of rivers we know are prone to flooding. And then we wail in anguish when a storm washes away everything we own. We want to blame someone, but instead of pointing the finger at ourselves, we blame God for not protecting us (*from ourselves*).

I am not God. I'm someone who has been touched by God's grace, thanks to the power of faith. Only He knows whether disease and disaster are meant to destroy us or *inspire* us to find a solution. Without challenges and obstacles, we become complacent. We need them in order to grow. Maybe we're not meant to know all the answers to the "Why me, why now?" questions. Maybe all we're meant to do is look for what each challenge means to us in the moment, and then ask, "What now? How can I use this to somehow benefit me and my future? How can I turn this around and use it to serve the world?" It's up to us to become responsible. It's our job to be the change that we seek.

BE GRATEFUL

Be grateful that you don't already have everything you desire.
If you did, what would there be to look forward to?

Be grateful when you don't know something
for it gives you the opportunity to learn.

Be grateful for the difficult times.
During those times you grow.

Be grateful for your limitations
because they give you opportunities for improvement.

Be grateful for each new challenge
because it will build your strength and character.

Be grateful for your mistakes.
They will teach you valuable lessons.

Be grateful when you're tired and weary
because it means you've made a difference.

It is easy to be grateful for the good things.
A life of rich fulfillment comes to those who are
also thankful for the setbacks.

—AUTHOR UNKNOWN—

CHAPTER THREE

GRATITUDE
More Than "Thank You"

"Gratitude unlocks the fullness of life. It turns what we have into enough, and more. It turns denial into acceptance, chaos to order, and confusion to clarity. It can turn a meal into a feast, a house into a home, a stranger into a friend. Gratitude makes sense of our past, brings peace for today, and creates a vision for tomorrow."

—MELODY BEATTIE—

I heard a story about a man who carried a "gratitude rock" in his pocket. Every time his hand touched the lump he would think about something he was grateful for. Very shortly after, his life began to change, and good things started to happen for him. That man told another man about his experience, and then that man told a village. Soon the villagers were happier and healthier than before.

When I heard that story I couldn't help but want what they had. So I set out to find a "gratitude *something*" to put in my pocket. It didn't take me long to find just the thing: a small toy, koi fish staring up at me from our living room floor. (Coincidentally, the koi symbolizes courage, perseverance in adversity and overcoming life's difficulties, strength of purpose and the ability to achieve high goals.) Without much expectation I put the fish in my pocket and for the next few months made a conscious effort to touch it throughout my day. No matter where I was or what I was doing, I forced myself to think of something—*anything*—that I was grateful for in my life; past, present, or future. I began to mold my future by being thankful for how each thing or person had somehow benefited my life. *Very quickly*, my situation and overall outlook began to improve.

What Is Gratitude?

Gratitude is an automatic "vibration raiser." When you're grateful, you feel great and you do great things! More than any other emotional force on Earth, gratitude forces you to focus on the positive rather than the negative. In fact, it's impossible to feel grateful and negative at the same time. There will always be *some* aspect of every person, thing, or situation that we can feel appreciation for. Therefore, there is nothing stopping us from choosing a positive state of mind 24/7, if we so desire.

Like a form of anti-depressant, gratitude is a quick-fix solution which has the ability to automatically change the way you think and feel. But unlike the former, its positive effects are everlasting. The beautiful thing about this amazing "drug" is that we can *always* access it. There is no prescription you need to fill. There is no limit to how much you can take, or a specified time when you must take it. It's always available when you need it because it's always inside you, waiting to be used.

We've all been thankful for one thing or another; sunny days, the people we love, money, presents, or compliments. But how has "being grateful" changed *your* life? Maybe you answered that it hasn't. Maybe you see gratitude the way I used to—as nothing more than a sophisticated word for "thank you:" a passing thought of appreciation quickly forgotten. When you look at it that way, is gratitude really anything more than just a *word?*

Gratitude is a thought, a feeling, an action, and a way of life. For thousands of years, millions of successful, happy people all over the world have been using gratitude as a technique to increase their potential, build incredible wealth and success, strengthen relationships, ignite love, improve physical health, restore self-esteem, boost confidence, develop new opportunities, and strengthen their connection with God, all with the most remarkable results. It goes without saying; those who regularly practice gratitude are generally more fulfilled in all areas of their lives than those who do not.

In an article printed in *Successful Living* magazine, a claim was made about the effects of gratitude on health. "Psychologists Robert Emmons, at the University of California at Davis, and Michael McCullough, at the University of Miami, are foremost researchers in the emerging field of gratitude. What they have learned so far is that gratitude is good for you, *really* good for you."

Studies show that people who practice gratitude regularly experience many positive benefits; including better health, greater wealth, richer relationships, and increased happiness and confidence; not to mention lower levels of stress and depression, compared to those who don't (Justice 2007, 18-19).

Gratitude is the key to financial wealth.

There is no question about it, grateful people experience increased wealth. Gratitude is a real energetic force in the world. The more you are grateful for your existing wealth, the more you will find to be grateful for. The old expression, "the rich get richer and the poor get poorer," could be more accurately stated as, "those who *feel* rich get richer and those who *feel* poor get poorer."

Grateful people feel rich. Understanding the feelings of having a lot, they come to desire more of the same. They become enthusiastic and confident in their abilities to set and accomplish big (and small) goals. The more they accomplish and receive, the more they have to feel grateful about. It's cyclical (and thus the reasoning behind why goal setting works best when combined with the practice of gratitude).

Gratitude is the core of all spirituality.

The power of gratitude has a reach far beyond the tangible. It is your connection with a Higher Power. It connects us with God by creating a deep, emotional feeling of *faith* that reminds us we've been blessed; that our life is a gift to be cherished and fulfilled. Giving thanks is the simplest form of connection you can have with God.

"If the only prayer you said in your whole life was, 'thank you:' that would suffice."

—MEISTER ECKHART—

Gratitude is beneficial to your health.

It's a fact. Those who practice gratitude are physically and mentally healthier than those who do not. When we feel grateful, serotonin (our body's "feel good" chemical) increases, positively stimulating our immune system. Low serotonin levels are said to be the cause of many of our ills, such as depression, lowered sex-drive, anxiety, apathy, fear, anger, increased appetite and cravings, insomnia, and fatigue.

Gratitude is good for your heart and soul! Emmons and McCullough's research shows that when we think grateful thoughts, "the feeling that goes with the thought, the parasympathetic (calming-branch of the autonomic nervous system) is triggered. This pattern, when repeated, bestows a protective effect on the heart . . . This may not only relieve hypertension, but also reduce the risk of sudden death from coronary disease."

Gratitude is the key to personal growth.

The second you become grateful, your thoughts, emotions and attitude begin to shift. And the more you practice gratitude, the easier things will become. Your eyes will open up and you will awake to a reality which once eluded you—the one where you are in control of your life. Thoughts, feelings and situations which once baffled you will become almost effortless.

Gratitude creates faith, and with faith comes the excitement of more to come. As you start to look within (and to God) for the answers, no longer will you see your glass as being half-empty; in need of someone else to fill it. Instead, you will begin to see life as a precious gift; filled with endless opportunity. Day-by-day, the more you experience the miracle of gratitude, the more you will want to experience. You will want to change and grow. You will want to become the person God intended you to be.

Gratitude is the doorway to happiness.

Gratitude releases the flow of love, kindness, acceptance and serenity into our lives. It also has the power to inspire forgiveness and mend broken relationships and past hurts. It can turn even the biggest failure into an opportunity. Gratitude enables us to savor the gifts that already lie beneath our "Christmas tree" of life, when life is going well. And when things are going poorly, it allows us to see the hidden blessings in everything. With gratitude, financial struggles offer an opportunity to shift our priorities. A job lost is another chance to go after your dreams. Serious illness, or even death, offers the chance for family members to grow closer.

In Buddhism there is the expression; "turning poison into medicine." Every "poisonous" situation can be transformed into something medicinal, but only when we look at it through the eyes of gratitude.

Perhaps the best reason of all for unlocking the power of gratitude is that it feels wonderful. Feeling grateful is its own reward, even if it didn't provide a host of other miraculous benefits. Compare a moment of gratitude to a moment of complaining. There's no contest. Why anyone would choose to live without gratitude is one of the great mysteries of human life.

How to Be Grateful

In order to be grateful, you must determine what or who it is you are grateful to. Gifts are always given by a giver. So before we move forward, let's all agree that some Divine Source (other than your parents) has given you life. And I don't just mean your physical existence, but *everything;* all your talents, gifts and experiences, including the world around you. For this, and *to* this, you should be thankful. Again, not to sound repetitive, but for the sake of clarity, I have chosen to call this force God. You should choose whatever works best for you.

I've always found the saying, "Well, at least you have your health," to be a difficult pill to swallow. When was the last time you were struggling to pay your bills, but were grateful because you had your health? I know from my own experience that when the bank took away our home I certainly didn't feel fortunate or remotely grateful just because I had good health.

I'm not saying it's impossible to feel grateful for one's health. I *do* in fact feel extremely grateful to have a healthy body and five glorious senses for exploring this incredible world. What I am saying, is that gratitude is not something you feel, or pretend to feel, because you know you should be grateful. That's what I call "gratitude for the sake of gratitude." A "Thank your Aunt Mary for that nice yellow shirt," kind of gratitude. That's not real gratitude; it's manufactured. That kind of gratitude doesn't change anything because it's fake. It's *pretending* to be grateful because, as people are always telling us, "things could be worse."

People in general are empathetic creatures. Intuitively, we know when we're more fortunate than others. When we see a person confined to a wheelchair, a grieving parent, a victim of a disaster, or a friend in need, we instinctively know that we're blessed to have what we have. And yet, on a daily basis, we remain uninspired by our gifts. We prefer to whine, complain, and take our blessings for granted rather than allow them to do what they're meant to do, which is "bless us."

The question is; if we're so blessed, why do our own lives seem to pale in comparison to others? Why does the grass always seem greener on the other side? The answer is simple; because we don't know *how* to be grateful. Gratitude is a tool, an advantage—*a gift* which resides in all of us much like an undiscovered talent. It's there waiting to provide us all the health, wealth, love, success, and happiness we dream of. But we must first learn *how* to use it.

Understanding the Benefits

Here is where it all begins to make sense. Up to this point you may have been wondering what connection there could possibly be between gratitude and goal setting. It all comes down to this; whether we like to admit it or not, everyone has a "*What's in it for me?*" attitude. Everything we do, we do because we think it will benefit us one way or another. We even do the things we hate in order to gain acceptance and avoid pain or further trouble.

So it makes perfect sense that even something as sweet and as spiritual as gratitude would come down to personal gain. Even though it sounds self-serving, there is absolutely nothing wrong with being focused on personal gain, as long as it's not at someone else's expense. It's the way humans are programmed. We like to do things that make us feel good; we hate to do things that make us feel bad. And that's okay; God wants us to feel good. In fact, in His infinite compassion, He has designed a universe in which doing good *feels* good.

The feeling of gratitude may not come easily at first, especially for those who have never tried it, or who did so, but with limited success. Gratitude is easiest to muster, and most gratifying, when you recognize the value, or the benefit provided by those people and things you are attempting to be grateful for. Once you have established what or who you are grateful to, think of how you benefit from having them in your life. In other words, how *does, can,* or *will* they potentially improve your life? When you acknowledge the benefits (and there is always something), you will find a heartfelt *reason* to be grateful for them.

Understanding the actual *benefits* each person or thing has to offer will help you realize how blessed you truly are; bridging the gap between *trying* to be grateful and actually *being* grateful. That junky old car you hate. Does it have some benefits too? Of course it does. Maybe, for instance, it saves you hundreds of dollars in loan payments every month because it's already paid for. What does that extra money allow you to do? Buy a new car, maybe? Invest in real estate? Travel?

Here's how it works. When thinking of (or writing in your *Gratitude and Goals* Daily Journal about) something or someone you're grateful for, immediately come up with a specific reason *why* you are grateful for them. That *why* is your benefit. If someone asked you why you are grateful for your mother, for example, you might answer; *because her unconditional love and support has helped me become a confident, happy, and successful person.* Your mother is the *object* of your gratitude; her unconditional love and support is what she gives (the benefits) so that you can use them to advance your life (the reward).

Feeling grateful for what you have bears tremendous influence on your moment-to-moment wellbeing. It is the first step towards achieving a truly satisfied life. But if what you want is to start living passionately, you will need to take gratitude to the next level. This next step involves a bit more creativity and planning on your part.

Here is where you begin to use it *as a tool* to help you create the life you want and deserve. Ask yourself this question; "How can this benefit enhance my life?" Or better yet, "How can I take advantage of this benefit so that I can improve my life?" This is where gratitude meets goal setting to create a powerhouse of possibility!

For example; let's say you determined you were grateful for this book. Here's how you might use that gratitude to help advance your life in some way:

Step 1: State what you are grateful for.

"I am grateful for *Gratitude and Goals* . . .

Step 2: Determine the benefit(s).

. . . because it is teaching me how to turbo-charge my life via gratitude and goal setting.

Step 3: Envision the outcome.

The third step involves determining how you *can* or *will* use that benefit in order to improve your life. It requires you to use the power of imaging, or what I like to call "creation" thinking, to create the desired outcome, first, in your mind.

. . . With this knowledge, I will be confident and capable of setting and achieving even my biggest goals and dreams. I will make more money, achieve optimum health, have true love, and acquire inner peace and joy."

I know that example was a bit extreme, but hopefully you get the point. Gratitude is more than just a thought. It is your inspiration for wanting more and being more, but more important, it will give you the confidence to know you can have it, if you take action!

Step 4: Create the outcome

Set goals and accomplish them every day!

The fourth step goes beyond the feeling of gratitude and into action. It is about implementing a plan of achievement so that you can turn the image you have into reality. Again, that's something we'll discuss in subsequent chapters, but you can begin to apply it right away in your *Gratitude and Goals* Daily Journal.

When things turned upside down for my family a couple of years ago, I was not a grateful person. Not because I didn't have reasons to be grateful, but because I didn't *realize* I had reasons to be grateful. Once I figured out what those reasons were and began to focus my energy on ways to take advantage of the benefits rather than wallow in the pain, my life instantly began to change. It can change your life too, the moment you begin to focus on the benefits to a problem and then come up with a proactive solution to remedy it.

Just last week I was speaking to a group about gratitude. Afterwards, a woman approached me, thanking me for my talk. In our conversation, she mentioned that she probably *should be* more grateful for her certain things in her life, especially her job, *even though she doesn't get enough hours*. I could tell she either, a) had never tried gratitude, or b) had tried gratitude, but with little or no success. How could I know this? Let's dissect her comment for a moment to find the answer.

First, she said she "should" be more grateful. To me that was a sign that she was skeptical. She obviously didn't believe in the power of gratitude; if it has any power at all, right? I could tell she wanted more satisfaction, but doubted she would have given gratitude a try, even though she said she "should." So, I pushed forward.

I pointed out to her the one thing she had overlooked; the one thing that caused her grief—the fact that *her job wasn't giving her enough hours*. I suggested that maybe it was the one thing she should actually be grateful for, instead of perceiving it as a setback. Thanks to the extra time, she could now focus on other things such as her spirituality (which she claimed was important to her), physical fitness, or even creating the career of her dreams. If she gave it some thought I'm sure she would agree that it's because of this extra time that she was able to do all the reading and journaling she was doing, which she told me was very important to her as well. Sure, she could probably use the extra pay, but who says she couldn't make money elsewhere; doing something she really loved, during the down time her job provided.

This brings me to my second point. When you're attempting to be grateful, just *be* grateful, without attaching conditions to your gratitude (I can only be grateful for that thing or person if/when/even though, etc.). Using this same example, if this woman really wanted to be grateful for her job she would need to change her wording to something more like, "I am grateful for my job because . . ." That's it. No conditions. Not *even though they don't give me enough hours*, or anything else she could have found fault with at her job.

This goes for everything, no matter whom or what you are attempting to be grateful for. Gratitude is a form of acceptance. If you want to reap the rewards of being grateful, then simply *be* grateful. Venting, resenting, blaming, self-pity, or whatever negative feeling you may have about it/them are only going to hinder your progress towards enlightenment. There is a time and place for this kind of rehashing, but this isn't it.

Third, in every (perceived) negative situation, there is an opportunity for personal gain. If it's an opportunity, it really isn't a negative; but a positive. When you see the things in your life in terms of benefits rather than liabilities, your mind will open up to new possibilities and your existence will suddenly become very exciting. No longer will roses be background décor; they'll become colorful, fragrant blossoms that brighten your day. And no longer will a fight with your spouse be the end of the world, but rather an opportunity to become a better person and to grow stronger together as a couple.

If by chance, the woman from my example wasn't doing anything with that extra time but sitting around all day, then becoming grateful for it would definitely open her up to the amazing possibilities it offers. Once she learned how to be grateful, she could begin to use that time productively, to set goals and work towards bettering her life instead of complaining about it. When I pointed all this out to her it was as though a light went on. She was ready to start living gratefully.

Chapter Four

GRATITUDE
Yesterday, Today And Tomorrow

"To believe in the things you can see and touch is no belief at all.
But to believe in the unseen is both a triumph and a blessing."

—BOB PROCTOR—

Gratitude helps you live in the moment.
Gratitude helps you plan for the future.
Gratitude helps you heal the past.

Gratitude Helps You Live in the Moment

How often can you say that you really live in the moment? Living in the moment happens when one genuinely wants nothing more than "what is" at that moment; when one just accepts life fully on its own terms, without trying to judge it, change it, or escape it. If only we could all be that "Zen"! The fact is we all can be.

When we can stop long enough and separate the mind (in other words, turn it off) from the body, inner peace has a chance to set in. In that moment, we are able to feel fully, to love fully, to be grateful fully; to just *be*. Becoming free to appreciate, rather than criticize the world *exactly as it exists*, is the heart of spiritual enlightenment, and a life of pure joy. True gratitude comes in stillness. We think to feel (and even deciding *not* to think is a mental decision we make). When we think of something to the point of feeling, we pass over an invisible line into stillness. We feel in order to *be*. The state of being *is* gratitude for the moment.

Being present takes practice, just like anything else. It's funny, because the present is all we really have. Our body is always present; it is our mind which tries to escape us. Right now, as I type this, I am nothing more than a person moving her fingers on a computer. That's what an outsider would see and the fact is that it's all I really am. Often when I am trying to just *be* in the present, I quiet the mind and step outside myself. I see *me* as an outsider would. Since they cannot access my thoughts, to them I am nothing more than an empty, mindless figure. That's probably why so many can kill without remorse. They fail to see that inside each "body" is an ongoing chorus of thoughts and emotions. *People see us as nothing more than a physical "body"; we see ourselves as the world.*

In order to attract more of what you want (happiness, love, well-being, money, success), it's important to first show gratitude for the things that already exist. I don't just mean the usual things people tell you should be grateful for, like the roof over your head and "your health" kind of stuff, but everything and everyone that touches your life (including you). Start by taking a good, honest look at your life and noticing only what is present, not what is absent.

For every person, place, or thing, there is a reason to be grateful. See each person as a soul looking to be touched. True love can only be felt when we are still enough to enjoy it. Touch someone (with your hands or your heart), and just feel them, without thought or judgment. Give to them fully without thought of taking a thing in return.

❦

"Enlightenment means choosing to dwell in the state of presence rather than in time. It means saying yes to what is."

—ECKHART TOLLE—

❦

Take a few moments throughout your day to be grateful for even the smallest things. Put a gratitude "something" in your pocket and use it. Or take time out to write in your *Gratitude and Goals* Daily Journal. Finding reasons to be grateful shouldn't be a complicated task. Even on the days when life seems to be treating you unfairly, there are countless reasons to be grateful; a good hair day, a great cup of coffee, your children's laughter, your health (*especially* your health), the sunshine, the color of your eyes, the country you live in, your kids, your friends, your job, your talents, the money in your account, a good conversation, the gas in your car, the "moment," etc. Remember to think of the ways in which you can benefit from each one.

One afternoon while my youngest son and I were waiting at the dentist, I made a conscious effort to just live in the moment. I allowed myself to focus on nothing else but my baby; watching him closely as he devoured a fresh strawberry. Red juice oozed all over his face. I looked into his big brown eyes and saw a tinge of auburn there that I never knew existed. I lightly touched his arm.

His skin felt so soft. His tiny hairs tickled my hand. I probably touch him dozens of times each day, but this was the first time I had allowed myself to really *feel* him. What an amazing gift he is, I realized. I laughed in delight as he begged for more strawberries. *In that moment he was perfect. I was perfect. Life was perfect.*

Before long that precious moment was over. My mind started to wander into the next room where my older son was being worked on. I began to worry. Was he okay? Then I started to think about a bunch of other things I had to do that day . . . and my baby continued to eat his strawberries, unnoticed. *Sigh* . . . Oh well, it was only a moment, but it was ours. I'll never forget it. And for that I'm grateful.

Of course it's important to write goals and make plans, but no matter how hard you think and plan and strategize, you can never be in any moment other than this one. There is no past or future; there is only *now*. It is resentment of the past and worry about the future which makes us so unhappy. But neither the past nor the future is real! Only this moment is.

Instead of wallowing in self-pity about all that you don't have or haven't accomplished, be grateful for the many ways in which you're blessed today. This day; *this moment*, is the only one you really have. And it is missing nothing. Plan for the future, but live in the now; knowing that the way you choose to live today has an effect on tomorrow. Each grateful moment you embrace not only enhances your life right at this moment, but lays the groundwork for a more abundant future.

Gratitude Helps You Plan For The Future

Gratitude is a very powerful tool, which when utilized, *can* and *will* help you build the future you desire. How?

Gratitude inspires you to want more, to trust that there is more available to you, and to do more as a result.

A grateful heart is excited about the future and all its possibilities.

Gratitude gives you the confidence to make goals and consistently work towards their achievement.

When you're grateful about the good things you already have in your life, you live with confidence that more is to come, and have faith that it's on the way.

Gratitude keeps you centered; even when times are their toughest.

It keeps you thinking and moving forward, by putting you into a positive, confident, and faithful state of mind.

Understanding Faith

To best describe the type of faith I refer to in this book, I've chosen to draw on this Buddhist definition from Wikipedia.org:

Faith refers to a sense of . . .
- Conviction that something is
- Determination to accomplish one's goals
- Joy deriving from the previous two sensations

Let's take a closer look at that statement . . .

Faith starts with a conviction that something is.

Faith exists when you choose without doubt, to believe that God and the Universe *are* there for you. When you choose to believe this, then it becomes true. (It is true whether you believe it or not, but you shut out the benefits when you don't believe.) This conviction leads to . . .

A determination to accomplish one's goals.

When you believe you're guided by God, you have the confidence to create new goals; big or small. You work towards them, knowing that with God on your side, you can accomplish everything you're meant to do. Because you feel this way you have . . .

A sense of joy deriving from the first two sensations.

When you have faith that God is on your side, guiding and taking care of you, along with the sense of purpose and focus this provides, life will have meaning and joy. You gain peace of mind, knowing that whatever challenges come your way; you can not only handle them, but become stronger as a result.

Faith comes easiest to those who take time to acknowledge life's little miracles. It can all start with a single moment of clarity; one deep feeling of gratitude. Even this moment is a gift. Being grateful in this moment creates unswerving trust in the future.

Gratitude in Advance

I'm going to repeat this because it's worth repeating: what we do now will have a lasting effect on the future. For this reason, I give thanks for today, knowing that every positive thought I have, every lesson I learn, and every action I take, is creating a better tomorrow. This is called having *gratitude in advance*, and it is the ultimate act of faith. Taking time to be grateful *in advance* gets the message across (to God, the Universe and your subconscious) that you're sincerely appreciative of all the gifts you've been given and are excited about what the future holds.

⸙

"People who can sincerely be thankful for the things which they own only in imagination have real faith. They will get rich; they will cause the creation of whatever they want."

—WALLACE WATTLES—

⸙

Gratitude in advance may be the single most powerful "tool" there is for manifesting your deepest desires. If you can hold a picture in your mind of what you want, and back that desire with robust faith that it is being created by your thoughts, feelings and actions, you can truly put yourself in the "gratitude vibration" toward things that are not yet evident in your life. And you will have unlocked the deepest secrets of success.

After filing for bankruptcy, things declined quickly. One day I was driving a beautiful new truck and the next day I had to give it back because we couldn't afford the payments. I was left driving my husband's old car; the one he'd bought before we started dating. I despised that car! It was a two-door with rear wheel drive. Not the type of vehicle a stay-at-home mother of two would want to own. Every time I went to put my kids into their car seats, I literally had to jump hoops (and buckles) to get them inside.

Soon after I began to drive it, it started to make a loud, embarrassing noise. The driver's seat was stuck and wouldn't move up, and it seemed to always run out of one type of fluid or another. My husband swears it worked fine before I started driving it. He claims my negative energy toward it actually sped up its demise. You know, he's probably right. It really wasn't such a bad car.

My negative attitude towards that car was a reflection of how I felt about my life. When driving it, I felt bad about myself. I would wonder what I'd done to deserve such a rotten existence. I was intelligent, creative, and had great ideas, but here I was still driving around in this crappy car. And my husband and I were constantly broke, which put a strain on our marriage and family life. I resented my husband for our existence, but it was really lack of control over my own life that was the cause of my anguish. Desperate for a change, I put the only plan of action into place I could think of . . . I became grateful *in advance*.

Habit is the best way to burn something new into being, until it becomes your reality. By constantly rubbing the fish in my pocket I created a habit of gratitude, not only for the things that I had, but also for the things I *desired* and felt confident I *would* have. My life improved; on the inside and out. Instead of hating my husband's car, I chose to be grateful that it got me where I needed to go (most times).

Equally important, though, I became grateful for the car *I was going to have.* I would allow myself to *feel* the excitement of shopping for my new car, as if it was happening the next day. At the time I didn't know exactly how I was going to achieve my goal, but I could *feel* with every fiber of my being that I would be getting a beautiful new car soon. This enthusiasm gave me the confidence I needed to take action toward achieving my goal (we'll talk more about goal setting in the following chapters).

I changed my way of thinking and feeling by choosing to be grateful. Today I can honestly say that my marriage and I are stronger for the adversity we had to face. I made a decision to be in love with my husband again, to stop resenting him, to start looking at him with loving eyes, and to feel him with a loving heart. It was as simple as that—a decision!

Without this type of *in advance* gratitude, I don't know if I ever would have gotten past the dread of that terrible year. It made me excited about the future and the role I would play in changing it. *Gratitude in advance* will get you through the tough times by helping you look past the pain of yesterday and the struggles of today. It instills hope for a wonderful tomorrow. And, like all forms of gratitude, it feels good *right now.* The moment you stop fearing the future, and replace that with gratitude for what is to come, you feel your inner frequency shift. Life becomes joyful instead of wearisome.

The practice of being grateful *in advance* is a very powerful goal setting tool. It will give you the motivation to work towards the things you want; confidently knowing they're already being created by your thoughts and actions. The kind of gratitude I speak of here is proactive. It's not about sitting around waiting for your life to change so you can appreciate it. It's about acknowledging the tools you were given, and using those tools to change it. And how do you do that? Start by being grateful for them.

Does it sound as if I'm sending mixed messages? On one hand, I'm suggesting you become grateful for all you are and have, without complaint. On the other, I'm telling you to plan and pray for more. Are these two positions incompatible? Not at all.

Like you, I want to *have* more, *be* more and *achieve* more. Wanting more and being grateful for it in advance is not a sly way of making demands or expressing dissatisfaction with the present. It's an act of faith. God wants us to maximize our gifts and to experience as much of this garden of delights as we can. He also wants us to be grateful for what we already have. Without this type of gratitude, we will never truly know inner peace.

Many of us secretly think that if we fully appreciate everything we have *now*, we will lose our incentive to achieve more; we will become complacent. And so we go around in a constant state of dissatisfaction, thinking we are actually motivating ourselves into action. But that action rarely takes place, so all we really do is create a vibration of unhappiness. In that state, we never appreciate what comes to us; we only see what is still missing. Gratitude, in fact, attracts more and more things to be *grateful for*. We can be fully grateful for *this* moment, while also being fully grateful for the new things that are coming our way.

When you have faith in God and in yourself, and you take daily action towards receiving your desires, they will come to fruition. Being grateful in advance is your way of telling God that you appreciate the gifts He has given you and are committed to using them to their fullest potential.

Gratitude Helps You Heal the Past

As important as it is to be grateful for the present with all its blessings, and for the future you desire, it is equally important to be grateful for the past. Why?

We live in a world where everyone and everything is connected. Everything we do, think, and believe affects the world and others around us. The present state of the world we share is the collective result of *all* the past events that have occurred. Look at the environment. It didn't get the way it is all by itself. Each of us is responsible for its destruction and ultimately its repair.

People have the ability to affect one another in the same way. We are not alone in this world. We are all one; we are all connected. Each of us has the power to affect others by our words and our actions—*good and bad*. Everything we think, say and do affects everyone else, and the world around us. And in return, we are affected by others in the same way. In fact, we do most of our learning about ourselves by being with others.

Albert Einstein once said, "A human being is a part of a whole, called by us 'Universe,' a part limited in time and space. He experiences himself, his thoughts and feelings as something separated from the rest - a kind of optical delusion of his consciousness. This delusion is a kind of prison for us, restricting us to our personal desires and to affection for a few persons nearest to us. Our task must be to free ourselves from this prison by widening our circle of compassion to embrace all living creatures and the whole of nature in its beauty."

Some of the "worst" events in history have led to some of the most wonderful discoveries. The fact is, we can never look at any event in isolation and label it good or bad. Take the example of the All-American quarterback who shatters a bone on the football field. In the recovery process, he discovers a talent for acting. Ten years later he wins an Academy Award for Best Actor. Although painful at the time, do you think he considers his accident a tragedy or a blessing? I'm sure looking back at it he wouldn't change a thing, even if he could.

In our own lives, we often feel bitter about people and events in our past. We convince ourselves that something "bad" has happened to us, and is to be blamed for our current misfortune. We blame our parents, our teachers, past employers, ex-lovers, etc. In the end, everything that happened in the past is "good" because it provided us with an opportunity to change and grow. Gratitude includes being grateful for the "bad" as well as the "good." Gratitude for the past, including the most cruel and unfair things that have happened to us, means accepting that everything is connected and that every event, "good" or "bad," has helped to weave the tapestry of now.

Recurrent, concentrated negative thoughts about the past are dangerously powerful. If left unchecked, they can override all positive emotions, including love or happiness, take away your sense of control over your life and keep you from making any progress towards the future. They are the bondage which holds you in the past.

The past does not have to dictate the future. Being grateful for events and people of the past, even if only a little bit, will free you from the bondage of any pain they may have caused you. This will require a degree of self-honesty that you may not have tapped into until now. As painful as it may be to admit, everyone and everything you've ever come in contact with, including your worst enemy, has benefited you in some way. You are who you are today partially because of their influence, and for this you have reason to be grateful to them.

Make a conscious effort to let go of blame and resentment about the past. As long as you hold another responsible for the hurts you feel they've caused you, you are in fact nurturing suffering. It's like fanning a bed of flames, hoping they'll dissipate. You're hurting yourself; not them. It's been said that resentment is like drinking poison and hoping the *other* person dies. As soon as you recognize resentment of the past as something you created, then you will be able to take the steps necessary to move on.

Gratitude and Forgiveness

Forgiveness is not about cutting the *other person* slack. Forgiveness is something you do for yourself. People who forgive are happier and healthier than those who are not. Forgiveness has the power to release you from a lifetime of unhappiness and torment which has an adverse affect on your entire body. If you're filled with resentment against another, it's yourself you are hurting with your anger; not them. The other person probably doesn't even know how you're feeling. The resentment is in your head, not theirs. The "offender" probably sleeps better at night than you do. Does that seem fair? If not, what are you going to do about it?

Forgive. Let it go. Forgiveness is not a way of saying you *approve* of what the other person may have done to you. It is simply a way of letting it go.

"Peace is not merely a distant goal that we seek, but a means
by which we arrive at that goal."

—MARTIN LUTHER KING, JR.—

When times were toughest, I would lie awake at night, bitter about the misfortune my husband's business venture had brought us. I wouldn't even want to look at him sleeping peacefully while I twisted about, having my own private pity party. After a moment it would dawn on me that I had a choice as to whether to feel this way or not. I asked myself, *who's really getting hurt when I go into that dark place in my head? My husband, who's dreaming happy dreams? Or me, whose stomach is filled with knots?* And then it all began to make sense: The trick is a shift in thinking.

I began to make a conscious effort to be grateful. I would run through a mental gratitude list of all the things I like about my husband, including the support he gives me and how hard he works to make things better. I would become grateful *in advance* for all the good things to come, including an amazing future. By thinking only grateful thoughts, my anger would melt away instantly. I became relieved and at peace.

In forgiving another, you end up freeing yourself. It really has nothing to do with another person. You make a decision that you're no longer willing to suffer because of something that is past. The other person doesn't even have to know you're forgiving them, if you don't want them to.

Do you want to know how to stop being angry at someone?

I know this is going to sound crazy, but here it goes . . . pray for them. If prayer isn't your thing, be grateful for them instead. Praying sincerely for a person you consider a "thorn in your side" is one of the most powerful things you can do to break the old patterns of pain and bitterness in your life.

Try it. For a moment right now (or before you go to bed tonight), think about someone with whom you have a strained relationship. Give that person thirty seconds of your attention. Think about *how* and *why* you might be grateful for them. Forget they're the bad guy for a moment. Appreciate them for their good points (you might need to look at them from another person's perspective, if that's what it takes).

Remind yourself that "our enemies are our greatest spiritual teachers" and ask what lesson *about yourself* this person may be helping you to learn. Remember, everyone is put in your life for one reason or another. What is this person's purpose? What have you learned from your experience with him or her that's made you a stronger person? Or what can you learn if you open your mind and heart? If you're not certain, ask God: "*What am I supposed to be learning from this person?*"

Don't fight the process with negative thoughts. Even if just for the moment, allow old feelings of anger and resentment to fade and invite gratitude to move in. Truly *be* grateful, don't just say the words. Focus on at least one example of how this person benefited your life, even if it was just a lesson on how *not* to hold onto anger. If this seems like a tall order, then simply ask God to bless him or her as He sees fit. If you just can't bring yourself to do even that, then ask God to help you find the willingness to let your anger go.

Once you've done this exercise, stop and think about how it made you *feel*. Did it change the way you think about the other person? About yourself? If not, try it again tomorrow; and then the next day. Your resentment will eventually diminish and you will be free from the negativity that has imprisoned you for too long.

Forgiveness is simple, but not always easy. It's a process that often demands patience, persistence and relentless self-honesty. If you're lucky, you can forgive right away, but chances are it will unfold over a period of time. For me, forgiving the past has never been an overnight occurrence. Bit-by-bit, I've had to take down the walls; allowing old, hurtful thoughts and feelings to be replaced with new, more positive ones. The good news is that forgiveness is a skill. The more you do it, the better you get. Over time you learn to forgive faster and faster, so that the resentment never has a chance to take root in the first place.

Eleanor Roosevelt couldn't have been more right when she said, "Remember, no one can make you feel inferior without your consent." The next time you get angry with someone remind yourself that they don't control you. They don't have the power to make you feel anything you don't want to feel. You possess the absolute right to release the anger in an instant, or to hold onto it and let it fester. Only you have that control. It helps to remember that in the vast majority of cases, it was not the other person's intention to hurt you (and even if it was, that's not your problem). The "offender" is an imperfect being; as you are. You too sometimes hurt others without intending it. Remembering that can give you perspective and put you in a more forgiving place.

One other thing; we often hold onto our anger because on some primal level we don't like to admit that we *enjoy* it. We LIKE the feeling of having someone outside of ourselves to blame. We relish our righteous rage and don't *really* want to let it go. Until we are willing to examine the hidden "benefit" WE are getting out of staying resentful, we'll never really be ready to forgive.

Gratitude and Acceptance

Acceptance is basically the opposite of how you feel when you're filled with doubt, insecurity, impatience, disappointment, bitterness or fear. Acceptance is simply the act of recognizing something or someone just as they are, without judgment, prejudice or expectation. It's the resolve that no matter how hard you want to change it or them, that something or someone just "is" and that it's not your job to change it.

"Nothing is good or bad but that our thinking makes it so."

—WILLIAM SHAKESPEARE—

If you can love, and accept others as they are without judgment, expectation or attempting to change them, you will automatically rise above fear, resentment and insecurity. You will live in harmony with yourself and the world around you.

In any moment, acceptance is the sanest and most enlightened step a person can take. After all, what else can you do when there is *nothing* you can do? And yet, we humans seem to fight acceptance tooth and nail! One of the main reasons we fight acceptance is that we think it's synonymous with approval. If we *accept* something, we believe we are giving it our endorsement. "I can't accept things like rape, murder and war," we say. But acceptance doesn't mean we *approve* of something, it just means we recognize it as a reality. And only when we recognize something as real, rather than pushing it out of our consciousness through denial, can we deal with it realistically.

Another reason we fight acceptance, of course, is that once we truly accept an unpleasant fact as real, then we have to deal with it. When we *accept* people, insecurities and difficulties, we can stop resisting them and start *dealing* with them. We resist the need to fight it/them because we will have removed reasons for inner conflict; the *what if's, if only's, s/he should's* and *why me's* of the world. We will put down our guards and begin to create solutions instead of more problems. Only then will everybody win; including us.

Gratitude starts with acceptance. Gratitude is, in fact, the purest form of acceptance. Try to be grateful for something without accepting it first and you'll see how difficult a task that is. It's sort of like trying to cry and laugh at the same time. So, if you want to experience the joys and benefits of gratitude, start by accepting everything and everyone in your life.

CHAPTER FIVE

THE MORE YOU GIVE
THE MORE YOU WILL RECEIVE

"Thankfulness is measured by the number of words; gratitude
is measured by the nature of our actions."

—DAVID MCKAY—

To truly experience the abundance gratitude provides, we need to take our gratitude to the next level. We need to give back with true appreciation and respect.

In an article titled *Gratitude and Generosity*, Dr. Peter Dingle explains; "Research shows that serotonin levels (known as the 'feel good' chemical) increase, and your immune system is stimulated when you do an act of kindness or giving. You get the same effects if you observe an act of kindness or giving. That is why people who give, get pleasure, or as the Bible says, *'give and ye shall receive'* . . . The opposite is also true—greed and continually taking, leads to increased dissatisfaction, disharmony and poor health. Physiologically, it lowers serotonin and compromises your immune system."

It's one of the great paradoxes of reality—the more you give without expectation of receiving, the more you will receive. It's inevitable. Giving back to the world doesn't have to be a major ordeal. It doesn't even require much of your time or energy. It can be something as little as smiling at your spouse when he or she is having a bad day, using your God-given talents to create something, or a random act of kindness, like buying a cup of coffee for a complete stranger.

Communication with God comes in many forms. I do find purposeful prayer most effective when I am trying to work out a solution or am seeking wisdom. But when you are living your highest truth, when you are doing what you love, when you are creating with your soul, when you are doing for others and giving without expectation; *you are praying to God.* What if you gave a homeless man two ten dollar bills from your wallet, and he handed one to the guy beside him? What would you think? Would you be mad at him? Or would your heart be filled with love and appreciation for his act of kindness—a mirror image of what you had done?

We are closest to God when we *use* the gifts He has given us to better the world, as He would, with the intention of love, kindness and unity.

Here are a few suggestions for how you can show gratitude by giving back:

If you're grateful for the love in your life, give back love.

If you're grateful for your strength, do all things with confidence and conviction.

If you're grateful for the warm sun, go for a walk.

If you've been given a special talent, use it without delay. Bless the world with your splendor.

If you're grateful for good health, exercise, eat right and take good care of your health.

If you're thankful for your children, give them a life filled with love, attention and support.

If you love your job, go to work every day excited about being there, and give 100 percent.

If you're grateful for your family, tell them how much they mean to you.

If you're grateful for your future, live life to the fullest!

The power of gratitude can move mountains. But if you truly want to have more, to be more and to live the extraordinary life of your dreams, you have to be willing to *do* more. You have to be willing to give back to God, yourself and the world.

Starting now . . .

CHAPTER SIX

ON WRITING
A DAILY GRATITUDE JOURNAL

"You simply will not be the same person two months from now after consciously giving thanks each day for the abundance that exists in your life. And you will have set in motion an ancient spiritual law: the more you have and are grateful for, the more will be given you."

—SARAH BAN BREATHNACH—

N ow that we've laid the basic groundwork for the principles of gratitude, it's time to put them into ACTION. A daily gratitude journal is one of the very best ways to begin.

A gratitude journal is a place for you to acknowledge those you are grateful for, but more importantly, its purpose is to reshape your way of thinking, and ultimately, your life. It's been proven that people who write a daily gratitude journal (or "gratitude list") experience an immeasurable increase in happiness, hope, love, enthusiasm and success; vastly improving the overall quality of their lives.

Psychologists Robert Emmons and Michael McCullough recently held an experiment comparing people who kept gratitude journals with those who didn't. Their study showed that those who kept journals "exercised more regularly, reported fewer physical symptoms, felt better about their lives as a whole, and were more optimistic about the upcoming week . . ."

Their research has found that those who kept a gratitude journal "were more likely to make progress toward important personal goals; whether academic, interpersonal, or health-based. And young adults who practiced daily gratitude intervention (self-guided exercises) had higher levels of alertness, enthusiasm, determination, attentiveness and energy . . ." (Justice 2007, 18-19)

What Is a Gratitude Journal?

A gratitude journal is a daily inventory of the things for which you're grateful.

Whether you choose to start your day off on a positive note or end it with deep appreciation, a gratitude journal is guaranteed to get you into the daily practice of being grateful.

A gratitude journal helps you focus on solutions.

A daily gratitude journal will free you from the negative, allowing you to focus on solutions rather than problems. It inspires you to become proactive by setting and achieving new goals.

A gratitude journal creates results.

A daily gratitude journal makes you results-oriented by keeping you focused on your goals and accomplishments, rather than your failings. It helps you visualize outcomes and guides your plan of action.

A gratitude journal is personal.

A daily gratitude journal reveals your loving, adventurous, honest and fearless side. (Don't stifle your creativity for fear that your journal may be read. Find a secure place to hide it if this is your concern.)

A gratitude journal creates an "attitude of gratitude."

A gratitude journal is designed to help you get into the daily habit of gratitude. Continually look for things to be grateful for, and then write them down, until gratitude becomes habit.

A gratitude journal raises the vibration of your entire life.

The daily practice of gratitude will do more to raise your overall "life frequency" than just about any practice you can think of. Combine it with prayer and/or meditation to really turbo charge your inner *and* outer life.

By writing down what you're grateful for every day, you will begin to . . .

- Take responsibility for your life, your thoughts and actions
- Radically improve your outlook on your past, present and future
- Be inspired to take action
- Accept and forgive
- Live in the moment
- Shed fear and worry
- Love more; blame less
- Increase your overall confidence and courage
- Grow spiritually

A daily gratitude journal is an ongoing connection with your Higher Power. It's more than a list of things you are grateful for;

it's the foundation of a beautiful, spiritual journey. The purpose of a gratitude journal is to reshape your way of thinking, and ultimately your life, by replacing old, negative thoughts with a new attitude of gratitude. Once you've adopted the habit of gratitude you will know the kind of ongoing serenity, peace, love and joy that you've always craved but perhaps never knew how to obtain. And it takes only few minutes each day to achieve.

How to Write a Daily Gratitude List

A gratitude journal does not have to be completed at any particular time of day. Maybe you're the methodical type who prefers to write it in the morning as preparation for the day ahead. Or maybe you prefer to write it at bedtime after you've had a chance to unwind; to reflect on all that you were grateful for that day. And if the only time you seem to have to yourself is that half hour at lunch, then that's as a good a time as any.

In the *Gratitude and Goals* Daily Journal pages provided in the second half of this book (or go to **www.gratitudeandgoals.com** for a downloadable version), record four things you're grateful for every day. Even if you write the same thing day after day, that's okay. The important thing is to be grateful for something. I've heard it said: "*Bring your body; your mind will follow.*" Day after day, continue to write in your daily gratitude journal. Even if you have to force yourself to be grateful for something or someone, eventually the magic will happen. And before you know it, more and more things will naturally find their way onto your list and you will be filled with gratitude.

Here is an excerpt from my own *Gratitude and Goals* Daily Journal, listing a few of the things that I have been and continue to be grateful for:

Today I am grateful for . . .

1. My talents. Thank you for the many unique talents I've been given and the amazing future I am creating with them everyday. I wouldn't trade them for anything.

2. My kids. Thank you for blessing me with two smart, beautiful, healthy, happy children who make me laugh and smile everyday. They make life worth living.

3. Rainy days. Thank you for rainy days, which provide me the opportunity to stay inside and work on my book and get closer to completing it and receiving the rewards.

4. Insight. Thank you for the things that I'm constantly learning about myself; helping me to become a better, happier, more at peace person.

5. California. Thank you for allowing me to live in California where the beautiful weather energizes me and continually motivates me into action.

6. *Gratitude and Goals.* Thank you for the awesome future I am creating with my book and all the people I am helping with it.

7. My mother. Thank you for my mother and all the lessons I have learned from her. Because of these lessons, I have been able to find my own strength and follow my dreams with confidence and determination.

This is the format that works best for me. How you choose to write your list is totally up to you.

Here are a few simple things to remember when writing in your gratitude journal:

Write positive things only.

This is not the place for venting, blaming, whining, or complaining. Nor is it the place for justifying and rationalizing. This is a place for gratitude; pure, simple and unqualified! Remember, your outer life reflects your inner life, so it doesn't make much sense to be giving energy to the negative, especially here.

Write definitively.

Be clear and confident about what you're grateful for. No *ifs, buts, sort of's, almost's* or *maybe's* should make it onto your list. No half-heartedness is allowed. If you waver, you won't fully reap the benefits of gratitude the journal provides.

Focus on the benefits.

The purpose of a gratitude list is to inspire you to notice the positive in all things. Doing this regularly will fill your life with more of the good stuff and leave less room for the bad. Commit to finding the *benefits*—the ways each person or thing has enhanced your life. This is where gratitude becomes real and personal growth begins.

As you write, really feel the gratitude. Remember, gratitude is more than a word. Don't just write down the things you are grateful for, but create the experience of being grateful by feeling grateful for them. Gratitude journaling is nothing but an empty ritual if you don't truly experience the gratitude.

Create a routine.

Writing in your journal at the same time every day will increase the likelihood of success.

I prefer to write my journal in the morning as a kick-off to my day. This helps me focus my gratitude not only on the things I have, but also the things that I am *anticipating* having and am creating, in conjunction with my daily goals. Shortly after I wake up, I make a cup of coffee, sit down at the dinner table with pen in hand and let it all flow. Usually my kids are bouncing around, looking for ways to interact with me, and I'm filled with gratitude for all the ways they enrich my life. I often add them (and that cup of coffee) to my gratitude list.

My approach is to (1) list the thing I am grateful for; then (2) create a statement giving thanks to God for it/them. I always give thanks for at least one thing I *have now*. I also make sure to be grateful *in advance* for at least one thing I *intend to have*. When I give thanks for what I want in advance, I do so with complete confidence. With each word, I know I'm attracting that result into my life. Finally, (3) I make the effort to write down *why* I'm grateful for each situation, thing or person; focusing on how they *benefit* my life.

Try to include all three steps in your statements (the *object* of the gratitude, the *giving* of the gratitude and the *benefit* of the object); especially the last one. This is when gratitude starts to feel real, giving meaning to each item on your list.

If you're new to the idea of gratitude journaling and don't know where to begin, here are a few suggestions to get you started:

- If you're struggling with someone or something in your life, that's always a good item to add to your list. Write something you're grateful for about that person, thing or situation. Find the hidden benefit you may be missing. Ask what the person or thing has given you, even in an unintended way. Don't concentrate on the pain; just the benefits. Day-after-day, continue to add this troublesome person or circumstance to the list until your struggles disappear. I know it may seem like a tall order, but if you do it, you will see that it works.

- The *second* thing in your gratitude journal might be something you're grateful for about yourself. It could be your beautiful smile, your generosity, your talents or your Ph.D. It's all good. And don't forget to mention how each quality benefits your life! You have so much to offer, but may not know or feel it. By being forced to look at the things you're grateful for about yourself— physically, mentally, spiritually, etc.—you will learn to love and appreciate yourself more and more each day, and so will others.

- Be grateful for at least one thing you desire *in advance*.

- The rest of the list is totally up to you. If you're grateful for more than four things, then write more, but always try to write at least four, no matter what.

As the months pass and you fill your journal with blessings, an inner shift in your reality *will* occur. I promise. You'll be delighted to discover how fulfilled and hopeful you feel. Your outlook will change and a new sense of fulfillment will unfold. What *is* this new sense of fulfillment? It's your attitude of gratitude at work, transforming your dreams into reality!

But gratitude doesn't stop at your list. Make an effort to practice gratitude throughout your day. I've found my gratitude list to be a great start to my day. It clears my brain of any negative thoughts and focuses me on the day ahead. My gratitude list is the backbone of my goals, reminding me what I can do and what I need to do to achieve each one. Ongoing gratitude has also been the best overall remedy for all my mistakes and insecurities.

You can write more than four things to be grateful for each day. You could write more than fifty, I'm sure, if you gave it some thought. Do the journal, but nothing keeps you living in a positive, productive place like the constant practice of gratitude. Get something to put in your pocket, tie a string around your wrist, wear a medallion around your neck, or *whatever*. Touch it as often as possible, making a conscious effort to be grateful for something in that moment. Nothing will get you into the mindset and habit of gratitude faster than this. And before you know it, you won't even have to think about being grateful; it will become as natural to you as breathing.

CHAPTER SEVEN

INTO ACTION
Setting And Achieving
Gratitude-Driven Goals

"I believe that life is constantly testing us for our level of commitment, and life's greatest rewards are reserved for those who demonstrate a never-ending commitment to act until they achieve. This level of resolve can move mountains, but it must be constant and consistent. As simplistic as this may sound, it is still the common denominator separating those who live their dreams from those who live in regret."

—ANTHONY ROBBINS—

You can be grateful without setting goals and you can set goals without being grateful. People do both all the time. People fail at both too. The combination of enduring gratitude with goal setting is a powerful way to create lasting results. It is the quickest and best success formula available. The combination is so intense that it can actually begin to transform your future immediately. And that is why they've been put together in one powerful, action-packed format—the *Gratitude and Goals* Daily Journal.

Here's how it works. Gratitude (*in advance*) is an act of faith. Faith creates a sense of confidence that you are *deserving and capable* of having what you desire. Just as with gratitude, goals are more powerful when created with faith. The practice of *gratitude in advance* creates this belief. Even though it hasn't happened yet, having appreciation for something in advance allows you a glimpse of what life will be like once you receive its benefits. This glimpse will give you the enthusiasm to want to set and work toward goals with confidence that what you are doing (and thinking) now is making it all come true.

Build toward the future by working through your goals today. Know that through your thoughts and actions you are making them happen. How great would it be to have the life you always dreamed of? Dream big! As long as your dream is backed by action, it's no longer just a dream, is it? The practice of gratitude creates a shift in the way you think and feel. It replaces negative emotions with positive thoughts and feelings. It lifts your life frequency to a whole new level. But the world won't hand you the fabulous life you dream of just because you've found spirituality and a more positive attitude. I wish it were that easy! No, it's not enough to think positive thoughts; you must become willing to *do* things that support your new outlook if you are to achieve your desired results. In other words . . .

You Must Be Willing to Take Action

"Faith without works is dead."

—JAMES 2:20—

This book will guide, instruct and inspire you to take action, but I can't promise that you'll achieve any real benefits from simply reading it. You must be willing to apply these principles to your daily life. Positive thinking must be followed by positive *action* if it's to be effective. Action stirs the pot, shuffles the deck and sets in motion the thoughts and plans that would otherwise remain locked up in your imagination.

Does this routine sound familiar? You come home from work feeling too tired to do anything. You plop yourself on the couch and settle in for a night of your *new* favorite activity—watching TV. New favorite activity, you may be saying?

Think back. *Way* back perhaps, to a time when you didn't work so hard. You probably enjoyed more of what life had to offer then—friends, romance, adventure, spontaneity—and were enthusiastic about a future filled with endless opportunity. Then somewhere along the way, life took hold and brought you down a notch or two. You got tired, probably gained a bit of weight. You fell into a daily routine, lost your enthusiasm, and TV (or some other filler) became your new favorite activity. Sound familiar? If so, don't worry, you're not alone.

Day in and day out, most people wake up, go to work, come home, eat dinner, watch TV, then go to bed; tired from a busy day. They hand the steering wheel of life over to others, renouncing control over their destiny and then complain about the ride. They're not happy with their status and hope that someday things will get better, but secretly doubt they ever will. They succumb to the idea that this is how life is meant to be. They're forever destined to be a worker bee and nothing more.

Life isn't meant to be lived this way. But how do we break the cycle?

Become a doer! Start by setting goals.

Goal Setting: How It Works

Goal setting works. Studies show that having a goal vastly improves your overall performance at just about anything. When we don't know why we're doing what we're doing, we do it with half a heart. When we don't know what we want to do, chances are we'll most likely end up doing nothing at all. A goal provides an all-important sense of purpose and direction. It makes every action meaningful.

Maybe you want to improve your marriage, job or relationship with your kids. Maybe you want to start your own business. Maybe you just want to lose a few unwanted pounds, or maybe you want something bigger, like colossal fame and fortune. No matter what it is you want; big or small, you can achieve it by setting specific goals to help you.

What is a goal?

A goal is a purpose, a target or an objective.

It's something you aim to achieve either now, in a day, week, month, year or even twenty years.

A goal gives you something to look forward to achieving.

It brings meaning and passion back into your life.

A goal establishes your priorities.

It motivates you to focus your efforts on the important things that will help you get what you want out of life, instead of aimlessly spending your time on pointless tasks, to-do's and other distractions.

A goal gives you focus.

When you create a goal, the "why" you are doing a job has personal meaning to you and you will tackle each goal related task with full presence of mind.

A goal keeps you committed and determined.

It reminds you to ask whether each decision you make and each task you undertake is moving you closer to your objective or further away from it.

A goal provides a road map to take you where you want to go.

Each completed goal gets you closer and closer to achieving the life of your dreams (your vision for the future).

A goal, once met, gives you a sense of mounting accomplishment. Meeting goals gives you a sense of increasing momentum and confidence to try bigger and better things.

A goal takes an idea and turns it into action.

A goal transforms vague ideas into day-to-day reality.

A goal gives you something to work towards.

Only by making new goals and working towards their achievement will you know if you are headed in the right direction. If not, you can tweak your next goal and aim it in a truer direction. Remember, even in failure, if you learn something new, you win.

A goal inspires others around you to set and achieve goals too.

Everybody becomes a winner.

Goals are meant to focus you by prioritizing your activities. Paul J. Meyer, considered by many to be the father of goal setting (and the author of the foreword for this book), has been quoted as saying, "Writing crystallizes thought and thought produces action." Having a written goal will make you a more organized, more accountable, and a more committed person simply by reminding you of what *needs* to be done. But there is a difference between setting a goal and actually seeing it through to completion. Those who accomplish their goals do so because they are committed to them, from beginning to end. They persevere because they understand the most important factor determining their success; goal setting is about more than meeting an objective. It is a *process*.

Chapter Eight

GOAL SETTING AS A PROCESS

"Action is the real measure of intelligence."

—NAPOLEON HILL—

G oal setting is not a written affirmation you read aloud to yourself over and over again every day in hopes it will come true. And it's not a one-off type of thing you write down, then pin to a board and forget. By definition, a goal is something you *aim to achieve*. Goal setting is more than an objective. It is a *process*. It's the determining of "what" you want to achieve, "why" you want to achieve it and "how" you plan to achieve it. It's something you develop, fine-tune and work toward over time and with steady progress. And as such, it should be an exciting, fulfilling and forgiving process.

People often give up on their goals because they fear one little word: "how." When faced with the question of "*how*" they're going to achieve something, they are overcome with fear of what they *don't know*, instead of focusing on what they do know. They become overwhelmed with the enormity of the task, thinking they have to have it all figured out, right from the starting gate. Ultimately they give up—another failed attempt; another reason to believe they'll never be one of the lucky ones who get to live the good life.

What they don't understand is this; goal setting is a self-teaching and self-correcting process. The most important thing is to *start* and make a determination to *finish*. Everything in between will work itself out as you go; as it's meant to be. You can trust that the process will get you there, *if* you're committed to seeing each goal through to completion. And each goal met will help you achieve the next goal, and then the next and so forth. You learn not from the outcome or objective, but from the process of doing; leading you to the outcome.

Don't let the details of *how* you're going to accomplish something prevent you from even starting. In fact, you don't have to know everything (or *anything at all*) when you're starting out. What's most important is understanding *why* you want to achieve your goal. As with gratitude, knowing how a goal, once achieved, will benefit your life, greatly increases the chances that you'll stick with it until its completion. For example, if you were told that if you hit your yearly sales quota at the end of the year, then you would receive a $25,000 bonus, I bet you'd work your butt off to hit it. But if your boss simply told you to hit it because it's good for the company, I doubt you'd become motivated enough to even come close to your target. There's simply not enough benefit for you—the *why* does not have a strong enough impact on your life to do so.

"Plan your progress carefully; hour-by-hour, day-by-day, month-by-month. Organized activity and maintained enthusiasm are the well-springs of your power."

—PAUL J. MEYER—

Have faith in your idea and take the necessary actions to achieve your goals by setting long term, short term, and daily goals, along with daily action steps (I'll explain these in the following chapters). The "how" will reveal itself through the doing. It might take a day or it might take two years, but as long as you hold fast to the desire and work the *process* as it's meant to be, with persistence and determination, the "how" will be presented to you. When you become passionate about your goals, your thoughts will align themselves with all things related to them. It will become evident just how much support and opportunity there is available to help you achieve them. And when a plan does become apparent, you'll be able to act on it without hesitation.

Day in and day out, as you work towards your goal, life will happen and things will inevitably change, including your plans and priorities. When they do, you'll need to reevaluate and readjust your goals to suit your new lifestyle or outlook. That's all part of the goal setting process.

Beyond Positive Thinking

People often say that thinking and speaking positively about something (e.g., saying "when" instead of "if") makes that thing more likely to happen. For example, it's better to say, "*When* I get the job." rather than, "*If* I get the job." Yes, a positive shift in words can help, but without action, they're just that—*words!*

Before I started practicing goal setting *as a process*, the only things I ever created were files of ideas, boxes of incomplete projects and a whole lot of debt. I tried the whole positive-thinking /positive-speaking thing and got zero results. I set *many* goals, but usually forgot about them, or quit before making any real progress. That's because *setting* goals and *engaging in the process* of achieving them are two very different things.

Gratitude was definitely responsible for helping me feel excited about my life again. But I realized that if I wanted to take control and change the way things were going, I had to do more than just give thanks. I had to take action, starting with writing this book. One day, just a few weeks into my new life and my new project, I began to feel overwhelmed. *What did I know about writing a book?* My progression slowed and I started to look at other things and ideas for other "projects" to occupy my time. I bet you can guess what happened next . . .

That's right; the gratitude journal hit the back burner. But I really wasn't surprised. See, racing head-on into things, then quitting, had always been my modus operandi. At the beginning of each project or job, I'd conjure up big visions for what I wanted my future to look like; how rich, famous and successful I would become and how much love and respect it would garner me.

I made a conscious effort to say positive things like "*when it happens*" instead of "*if* it happens." I would get all excited, do a ton of research, make a call or two and maybe even spend money we didn't have on samples or services (some of them very expensive) which I felt were absolutely necessary for my success. And then, about three weeks into whatever I was doing, I got bored, scared, uncertain, too busy (or whatever my excuse), and then quit. All the money, good will and effort I poured into it went up in smoke.

One evening I approached my husband, excited about my new project (the gratitude journal). Oddly, he didn't seem to share my enthusiasm. It was then that he turned to me and said something so simple, so painful and yet so true that it changed my life forever. He said, "Stacey, I believe you're capable of doing anything you set your mind to. But please, just finish *something*." Wow! So that's what he thought of me. As someone who never finished anything? After a brief moment of self-pity and resentment, his message sank in. And for the first time, I was able to see what others had already known—I was a big talker, but a poor performer.

I never seemed to be able to finish anything I started. No matter how badly I wanted to, I always ended up making excuses why I couldn't. It was as if I wore an elastic band harness that would let me run full out, but then snap me back as soon as I gained any momentum. My old belief system desperately wanted me to quit, while the newly empowered part of me was determined to succeed. This time it would be different. Now I was determined to show the world (including myself) that I could finish *something*. And so the battle ensued.

Then one day I was talking on the phone with my mother

about her newest, great invention. I became excited for her and asked what she planned to do with it. Her explanation led me to believe that she *didn't plan on doing much*. Like the rest of her ideas, it was going to sit on her shelf of great ideas and collect dust. I became frustrated by her apathy. *Why was she giving up so easily?*

I got mad; basically blaming *her* for the way I ended up. I felt that if she would follow through on an idea just once, then maybe I could do the same. After I got off the phone and came down from my self-righteous rush, I realized it wasn't her that I was mad at; it was me. It wasn't her fault I never completed anything. She had been nothing more than my mirror image. And I hated what I saw—*someone who always dreamed of having more and being more, but never did anything about it*. It was as though life was passing my mother by, and I was afraid the same thing was going to happen to me.

Although my father was more of a risk-taker who owned several small businesses throughout his life, he seemed to want to protect me from having to struggle, by encouraging me to choose a "safe" career. Subconsciously, I was suffering from an internal struggle. Part of me wanted to be a risk-taker; to do great things with my life. But the other part of me wanted to play it safe because I didn't feel I had enough experience or resources to achieve anything significant. Even though I felt destined for greatness, it was as if my genetic makeup destined me to fail.

A few days later it hit me. A realization so simple and yet so strong that it would forever change the way I did things. It wasn't my mother or my father who was holding me back, but *my own perception of myself based on my past experiences*. Choosing to take absolute full responsibility for my life, I declared: "I am not my mother, my father or anyone else for that matter. I am me. I have to do things in my own way and in my own time, if I want to be happy, fulfilled and successful." In that moment I was freed from the bondage of my past. I stopped blaming everyone for my faults and failures, along with the need to please anyone but myself. I took back control of my life by doing the one thing I knew would solidify my new attitude. I took immediate action!

I sat down with a calendar in hand and set my first short term goal to write for seven hours in seven days. I broke it down into smaller, more obtainable daily goals; to write for one hour each day, to get the job done. I overcame my doubts and fear of a lack of experience by reading and researching as much as I could. With each new day my confidence grew. I was able to overcome the things which had once paralyzed me; uncertainty, procrastination, a lack of time, laziness and any other setbacks that did arise, by focusing on just one day at a time.

More importantly, I was really excited about my goals, because for the first time I truly believed that I *could* complete whatever I set my mind to. The very best part of each day became that hour when I got to work on my goals. As selfish as that may sound, I cherished that time more than anything else, because I was doing something truly meaningful. *Something just for me.* Moment-by-moment, day-by-day, I continued to work this way. And that's how *Gratitude and Goals* was born.

From Conception to Completion

"You must be the change you want to see in the world."

—MAHATMA GANDHI—

Most goal setting methods fail because they place too much attention on timelines and end results, with very little focus on the *process* of achieving each goal. Because there is so much emphasis on the *when* instead of the *how* you will accomplish them, you end up with little more than the dream of what you want, without the how to make it come true. Having a clearly defined deadline is not the most important factor in establishing the success of your goals. It's the *process* which determines the outcome.

"A goal is a dream with a deadline." How does that quote make you feel? As though your dreams will expire unless you achieve them by a certain date and time? I don't know about you, but that concept makes me feel like a failure even before I start. Don't get me wrong, I believe having a deadline is very important for providing organization and a target. I just don't consider it nearly as important as the ongoing steps required (the process) to complete each phase of your goal.

Deadlines give your plan of action structure by giving you something to work towards, while at the same time giving you something to work from; they are the target, and they are also the first step in the planning phase. They are what a destination is to a road trip. Without a destination, there is no point in leaving the house. But once you know exactly where you want to go, you can begin to plan a course to get you there.

For example, if you want to lose weight, you stand a greater chance of success if you say, "I want to lose fifty lbs in twelve months" rather than, "I want to lose fifty lbs." Having a deadline would help you figure out what you had to do on a month-to-month or even a weekly basis in order to accomplish your goal of losing the fifty lbs. This way, all you really have to do is come with a plan to work towards losing about a pound a week and then figure out what you had to do each day to ensure you met that goal. Without the twelve month deadline, you would have nothing to aim for and really no way to calculate each step.

Having an *ideal* deadline is also important because it instills a sense of urgency. And without urgency, you might stay stuck in "someday, somehow" mode and run the risk of putting things off, and possibly never getting anything accomplished. But unless your goal actually has a predetermined deadline (i.e., you want to be at a certain weight for your wedding day so that you can fit into your dress or suit), timelines should be considered nothing more than an *ideal*. If you give them too much attention, they may distract your focus from what is really important—the immediate actions required to get started, and the continuous actions required to keep the momentum going until your goal is achieved.

I know that with my busy schedule, unexpected things tend to happen which keep me from my daily goals. For example, my goal was to complete this book within three months from the day I started writing. But with only one hour a day (give or take) to work on it, plus the many setbacks and surprises I've had to deal with along the way, it has taken me much longer to complete than expected; three years longer, actually!

Am I a failure because I wasn't able to meet my original deadline? Of course not! The book is done, isn't it? Can you imagine if I decided to scrap my dream just because I wasn't able to meet my self-imposed cut-off date? And yet, that's just what many who fail do. Why? Because they place too much importance on two things when setting a goal: 1) *what* they want to accomplish, and 2) *when* they want to achieve it, by paying very little attention to the *process* of actually getting it done.

"Don't let the fear of the time it will take to accomplish something stand in the way of your doing it. The time will pass anyway; we might just as well put that passing time to the best possible use."

—EARL NIGHTINGALE—

Once you've written your goals, it's most important to spend your energy figuring out what you can do *today* to set things in motion (i.e., Google for information, send out resumes, make a call, order a course book, put out that cigarette, book an appointment with a personal trainer, schedule a meeting with your boss, etc.), instead of trying to predict when you will have it accomplished by.

Make plans and set timelines that *inspire you into action*, not weigh you down. Take a moment and try to figure out how long you think it will take you to achieve your goals, based on your experience, timing and of course your level of commitment to it. But remember, it's just an estimate. If you end up missing your mark and don't actually complete your goal when you estimated you would, don't stress about it. Give yourself an extension and keep trying until you do get it.

The *Gratitude and Goals* Daily Journal

The personal development teachers, who write many of the goal setting programs available, seem to assume that you know exactly what you want and how you plan to accomplish it. So they don't get into the details of helping you figure out "how" you actually get the job done. Their methods aren't written for everyday people, like me, who suffer from doubt, inexperience, procrastination and poor time management. They're not written for those who've never successfully completed anything of major significance. And they're definitely not designed for those of us who get confused or frustrated, sometimes even to the point of tears, when we don't know what we're doing. I guess they must be written for that one percent of advanced folks who know exactly *what* they want and *how* to get it. (But, of course, those people probably don't even need to be reading books on goal setting.)

It doesn't really matter who you are or what you desire. If you want to achieve your goals—and of course you do or you wouldn't be reading this book—you must become committed to making steady, ongoing and inspired progress until your goal is complete. That's what the second half of this book, the *Gratitude and Goals Daily Journal*, is all about—simplifying the *process*—figuring out how to effortlessly accomplish all of your goals, big and small, from conception to completion; one step at a time.

Your goals should have a natural and gentle feeling of achievability as well as work comfortably with *your* lifestyle and schedule. They should not be so aggressive that they're going to overwhelm you and make you want to quit. For example, if you were trying to write a book, it's better to set a goal of writing one page a day and to *actually achieve* it than to set a goal of ten pages a day and give up after a week or two.

Once people get overwhelmed or disillusioned, they give up, or, worse, they don't try at all. It is better to actually achieve a goal, even if it takes a little longer than you hoped, than to continually set ambitious goals and fail to meet them. Small, daily chunks of action quickly add up. Weeks of procrastinating do not. What makes the *Gratitude and Goals* Daily Journal such a powerful goal setting tool is the fact that it's, well, *daily!* It focuses on steady, manageable progress; in other words, "how" you're going to get things done, one step at a time. It acts not only as your reminder of the goals you want to achieve, but as your daily plan of action to make certain you achieve them.

The *Gratitude and Goals* Daily Journal makes accomplishing all of your goals; big or small, easy, manageable and stress-free. It takes you through the daily goal setting process by keeping you on-track and focused on *what* you want to accomplish, and *how* you're going to do it, not only *when* it needs to be done by. It also encourages you to constantly reevaluate and rework your goals so that they fit into your lifestyle, not the other way around.

This is your life you're creating here, so planning it shouldn't be a scary thing! While most other methods have you write out your goal, then look at it every few days, weeks or months, the *Gratitude and Goals* Daily Journal will keep you accountable to your goals *every day*. When we set goals, then put them aside, only to return to them weeks or months later, they become abstract and intimidating. This is what causes problems such as fear and procrastination. But if goals are ever-present and we work on them *just a little* every day, they become an organic, exciting and rewarding part of our lives. And after a few weeks of practice, goal setting becomes a natural part of your life; not just daunting and distant promises you forget about the day after you've written them.

This is a very forgiving program. Every day, when you write in your journal, you will have another chance to work toward your goals and even alter them if need be. If for one day, one week or even one month you're not able to write in your journal, it's okay. As soon as you're able, get back into the rhythm of it by simply trying again the next day. It is not meant to make you feel bad, guilty or like a failure. It's designed to support you, regardless of who you are or what your lifestyle is.

CHAPTER NINE

TURNING THOUGHT
INTO OUTCOME

"In your life's defining moments there are two choices—you either step forward in faith and power or you step backward into fear."

—JAMES ARTHUR RAY—

It's easy to have a goal but it's quite another thing to see it through to completion. When you do, that's what I call a success. Success is not defined by what you have or what you do, but by your sense of completion. What is successful to one may not be to another.

I have a vision of what I'd like my future to be like. I may not be there now, but I feel like a success every single day that I work on my goals. In fact, if I were to die today I would feel completely at peace knowing that I did my very best to pursue my dreams, without giving up on them or myself. Success isn't meant to be a six month, a year or even a five year target. It's an ongoing process. It happens when it happens—*when you're prepared to receive it*. Preparation is more than a state of mind; it's a state of being. So, how do you become prepared?

Here's a simple formula created to help you create success in ALL areas of your life:

Gratitude + Goal + Faith + Persistent Action = Outcome

Step 1: Be grateful for what you have, and what you *will* have.

Step 2: Create a definite goal. Commit to it. Be determined to get it.

Step 3: Have faith that you will achieve your goal. *Know* that it's yours in the making.

Step 4: Do the *do* things. Open your eyes to opportunities. Don't hesitate to act on them.

Step 5: Stay motivated. Keep pushing even when things seem difficult.

The world doesn't wait for those who hesitate. The most important factor that differentiates highly successful people from the rest of the world is that they don't just talk; they *do*.

What You Do Today Will Affect How You Live Tomorrow

There are two general schools of thought on how goals are best accomplished; the bottom-up method and the top-down method. I believe in both. Let me explain . . .

In his bestselling book *The Seven Habits of Highly Effective People*, Stephen R. Covey explains Habit 2: Begin with the End in Mind. This habit is based on the idea that all things are created twice; first, as a mental creation, and then as a physical creation.

Start from the top by creating a *vision*. Your vision is the big picture of your life as you dream it to be. This is your purpose in life; what you want to stand for, have, be and do in the future.

Your vision is the foundation for *all* your goals and actions. It is your motivation—*what you work towards* every day of your life. This is summed up in what I call a vision statement (we will look at this in more detail in just a little bit).

Next, you will want to create *long term goals*. These are your one, five, ten or twenty year goals. They are the big house overlooking the ocean, the thriving business, the Swiss bank account, the happy family, and the everlasting romance—*whatever!* Together, your long term goals make up the jigsaw puzzle that is your vision.

Your long term goals are your greatest individual aspirations for your future. But if what you want is to live life to the fullest NOW, then having *short term goals* are a must. These are your next week, next month, year or project-based goals. Finishing a book, running a marathon, losing thirty pounds . . . these are the things which will improve your outlook, your health, your lifestyle and your confidence NOW. They are also the actions you need to take today to get you closer to the tomorrow of your dreams (your vision).

No long or short term goals can ever be completed without *daily goals*. These are the day-to-day commitments you need to carry out if you plan to realize all of your short term goals. These are the things which build you up, make you wiser and stronger, and create constant progression towards all other goals.

Last, but probably the most important, are *action steps*. They represent a plan of action—the "how" of accomplishing your daily goals. Action steps are the moment-to-moment, hour-to-hour actions that you are required to complete throughout the day, in order to achieve your daily goals. Action steps will set you in motion, put you on track and keep you focused. Even the smallest bit of *real progress* is infinitely better than empty fantasizing and promises. Action steps are the reason you achieve *all* of your daily goals.

No matter what you want to accomplish, you can do it when you set manageable goals. Think of your goals as building blocks. Block-by-block they stack up on top of one another; building and building, until one day you've built a tall tower. Your vision is the motivation behind wanting to be successful, but the process of getting you there is driven by the smaller stuff. When establishing your goals, you must certainly look to the top by developing a clear, mental picture of what you want for your future. But all action must start from the bottom and work up to get you there.

⁘

"Watch your thoughts, for they become words. Watch your words, for they become actions. Watch your actions, for they become habits. Watch your habits, for they become character. Watch your character, for it becomes your destiny."

—UNKNOWN—

⁘

You can achieve almost anything you desire; one step at a time. You will be amazed at how quickly those steps add up. By taking the time-pressure off, you actually get things done faster. Before you know it, you will have the semester of school, the first draft of your book or your business plan completed.

When you work through the program as outlined here, understanding that each success is something to feel great about, your confidence will grow, you will become inspired and your enthusiasm will bubble over into your everyday life. All the success of goal setting will be yours, without pressure or the uncertainty of not knowing how to get it done.

If you want to create a goal that is not only exciting but very obtainable, make sure it is S.M.A.R.T: Specific, Measurable, Attainable, Realistic and Timely. (The origin of the S.M.A.R.T acronym is unknown, but has been referenced by just about every major player who has ever had success with, or taught goal setting, including Stephen Covey, Brian Tracy, Paul J. Meyer and Zig Ziglar.)

Goals should be specific and measurable.

Write exactly what you want to achieve, how much of it you want, how you're going to achieve it and when you are going to achieve it. Vagueness will get you nowhere. The clearer you are when writing them, the greater the chance of them being accomplished. Life changes, and so should your goals. Be flexible and forgiving of yourself. Make changes and adjustments as needed and you'll find goal setting more manageable and enjoyable.

Goals should be attainable and realistic.

To say, "I'm going to have my Ph.D. by the end of this year," is neither attainable nor realistic, especially if you don't even have a college degree. Write a goal you can truly obtain. Don't set yourself up for failure by setting a goal that is impossible to reach within a reasonable time frame. Remember, goals are like building blocks. Start small and continue to build up to larger and larger goals, until one day you realize your vision. Harmonize ambition with practicality. This will take some tweaking from time to time.

Goals should have a (flexible) deadline.

Have an ideal target date for completing your goal. If you do not meet that target, though, don't beat yourself up. Life happens. Your goals should be able to work with your life, not the other way around. If you do miss the mark, simply create a new one and continue moving forward without delay.

Create and sustain the habit of goal setting by writing them at the same time every day.

Habit is especially important when it comes to achieving long term success. What's the point in only creating one goal and achieving only one victory? Success isn't one win, but a compilation of wins, steadily building one after another. Once you achieve one success, it's only natural to want to have more! But goal setting, like any good habit, can quickly be forgotten if it's not part of your everyday routine. Plan to make goal setting part of your everyday routine for continual, and more importantly, *escalating* success.

It doesn't really matter when you choose to write your goals, as long as you attempt to write them around the same time every day. Do what's right for you. I prefer to write mine in the morning because it thrusts me right into plan of action. If you'd rather write them at night before going to bed, that's okay too. Just make sure to review them again the next morning. This way you will know how the rest of your day should look and be reminded of the things you need to get done. However you choose, creating a regular goal setting routine will develop and then maintain your goal setting habit for many years to come.

So . . . if what you want is to create goals that are not only exciting but very obtainable, *and* you want to ingrain the habit of goal setting into your long term memory in order to create long term success, then make sure your method of goal setting is not only *smart* but S.M.A.R.T.H:

Specific, Measurable, Attainable, Realistic, Timely *and* Habitual.

What's Your Motivation?

Mistakes are a great way of learning what *not to* do, but a lot of time, money and stress can be saved if you put some honest thought into your goals before attacking them head-on. Donald Trump says, "You have to love what you do. Without passion, great success is hard to come by." (Casey and Mann, 2008, 61) Be brutally honest with yourself. Know what it is you really want, not what you think you *should* want or what someone else is telling you to want.

Only visions and goals that are true to your heart will withstand the test of time and effort. It may take some soul-searching on your part, but once you know what you really want, going after it will be much more exciting.

Do What You Love

Here's a thought. Just because you may have many interests, it doesn't mean you have to do them all at once. The most successful people focus their energy on one thing at a time, mastering each thing before moving on to the next. By contrast, some of the hardest working, albeit unsuccessful people, make the mistake of constantly juggling several projects at a time. They start more projects in one year than most do in a lifetime and yet, never actually complete anything.

Here's another thought. Just because you're good at something, it doesn't necessarily mean you have to do it for a living. Many people become trapped by their own abilities. They become lawyers or accountants because they have a knack for logic or numbers (and of course the salary is pretty good, too). And then they spend a lifetime of regret pining for the true desires of their heart. That's not to say you can't be a lawyer or accountant and love what you do. You can. But loving the *trappings* of success is simply not enough.

It's been proven that when you're doing what you love you'll be happier than you would be making millions doing something you don't love. When we do what we love, we're excited, energized, focused and happy. We get into "the zone;" that place in our head where we lose track of time and become one with the action we're performing.

A few years ago, I decided to start my own linen company. I worked long and hard putting together the best possible designs, manufacturers and marketing. The day finally came when all my work was about to pay off; I was asked to design and distribute linens for a boutique hotelier. This is what it's all about; the big deal, the money, the recognition and the business. But instead of diving right into it like most normal people would have, I chose to step back and reevaluate what I was about to get myself into.

Yes, I did work very hard and I did borrow a lot of money to start the business. But in order to take this next step, even more time and more money would need to be spent. Would it be worth it? To many, the answer is, "Of course!" It just wasn't that straightforward to me. Although it all could have been very satisfying financially, it would have been a burden on my soul.

See, I've known for years that I wanted to be a writer (a creator actually, and writing is the medium I am most comfortable with), but because of the flaky stigma imposed on the profession, I thought it was safer and more prestigious to own a business. Instead I listened to logic—what my brain was telling me to do. (The analytical side of our brains is a wonderful tool for solving specific problems, but is a poor life manager. For managing a life, the heart must be consulted.) At the time, it seemed unfortunate that I would go so far with my company, only to quit. But the way I see it, it was a necessary learning experience which convinced me to finally commit to my life's passion. I had already wasted many years ignoring what my heart was urging me to do.

***

"Success in its highest and noblest form calls for peace of mind and enjoyment and happiness which come only to the man who has found the work that he likes best."

—NAPOLEON HILL—

***

It's never too late to do the things you've always wanted to do. In his landmark book, *Think and Grow Rich*, Napoleon Hill wrote that people don't generally become wealthy until they're in their forties. Those who succeed earlier should consider themselves lucky. Well, I'm thirty-seven years old. For some of the things I'd like to do (or would have liked to do) that makes me rather old. But the way I look at it, I have at least thirty good years of work ahead of me, so I might as well spend them doing what I love. The more I like what I am doing, the more money I will make and the less stress I will have. And as a result, the longer I should live to enjoy it.

Is the vision you hold really yours, or are you chasing someone else's dream? This is *your* journey. Not mine, not your mother's, your husband's, your boss's, your wife's . . . Traveling the globe on a yacht might seem like a great idea to your spouse, but if it's not equally exciting to you; it's your *spouse's* dream, not yours. There's nothing wrong with having a shared interest. That can be a magical thing. But no matter how hard you try, you'll never be happy living a lie.

I've always said that the best investment anyone can make is in themselves. Be totally honest with yourself when creating your vision. It's important to your soul that you use some of your time here on earth to nurture your dreams. What do you need to do, to have or to be before you die in order for you to feel complete? Listen to that inner voice begging to be heard. It's your true self waiting to be acknowledged. Listen to the voice and do what it says. It'll never steer you wrong.

Turn Your Dreams into Reality

When the day comes and you're about to draw your final breath, what will you think when you look back on your life? Did you become the person you wanted to be? Were you happy? What impression did you leave in the minds of those who knew you? Were you an inspiration or a drain? A model to emulate or a cautionary tale? What will be your legacy to the world and to those closest to you? Will you be proud of your decisions? Will you be fulfilled by your accomplishments and successes? Will you have any regrets? If so, what might they be? How might they be avoided?

This is your life. How you choose to live it is up to you. You can continue to look to others to make you whole, then complain and blame them when they fall short of your expectations. Or you can begin *today* to live the magnificent life that God intended for you, with the talents and courage He gave you to work with.

This is *your* life. How do you want to live it?

A Vision Statement

A vision statement is a powerful description of the dream you hold in your head and heart. It encapsulates your joy in life in all of its main areas; including career, lifestyle and relationships. It also takes into account your physical, mental, emotional and spiritual needs. A vision statement is not something you create to gain the approval of others, but a heartfelt, "If I could do, have or be anything in the world, in [x] years, what would that be?"

On August 28, 1963, Martin Luther King, Jr. made his famous

I Have a Dream speech. In his address, Dr. King set out his vision for an America liberated of discrimination and inequality.

> *"... I say to you today, my friends, so even though we face the difficulties of today and tomorrow, I still have a dream. It is a dream deeply rooted in the American dream.*
>
> *I have a dream that one day this nation will rise up and live out the true meaning of its creed: 'We hold these truths to be self-evident: that all men are created equal.' ...*
>
> *... This is our hope. This is the faith that I go back to the South with. With this faith we will be able to hew out of the mountain of despair a stone of hope. With this faith we will be able to transform the jangling discords of our nation into a beautiful symphony of brotherhood. With this faith we will be able to work together, to pray together, to struggle together, ... to stand up for freedom together, knowing that we will be free one day ....*
>
> *... And when this happens, when we allow freedom to ring, when we let it ring from every village and every hamlet, from every state and every city, we will be able to speed up that day when all of God's children, black men and white men, Jews and Gentiles, Protestants and Catholics, will be able to join hands and sing in the words of the old Negro spiritual, 'Free at last! Free at last! Thank God Almighty, we are free at last!'*

With his powerful vision, Dr. King inspired a nation into desegregation and prompted the 1964 Civil Rights Act. In 1965 he was awarded the Nobel Peace Prize. Today Americans continue to steadily change their ways of thinking and conducting their lives, thanks to Dr. King's tenacity.

Now it's your turn . . .

How to Write a Vision Statement

There's no single way to write a vision statement. It can be written in sentences or in bullet-point form. It can be stated poetically or matter-of-factly. It can even be created visually if images are more powerful than words for you. In fact, because it's personal, you don't even have to write it; it can be an audio recording.

A vision statement can be:

- a written essay
- a poem
- a drawing
- a cut-and-paste scrapbook or vision board
- a tape recording
- a video or film
- just about any other method you're comfortable with

A vision statement isn't meant to be safe; it's meant to be honest. Be true to yourself, your dreams and your desires. Remember, God does not ask you to play small. You are huge. And so is your potential. Know that there's no such thing as a dream that's too big, a desire that's too strong or an idea that's too extreme. The world wasn't built by those who played it "safe" but by those who were courageous and "extreme." Be courageous! Be "extreme"!

Not sure where to start? Here are some areas in your life you may want to improve:

- Talents/Hobbies
- Finances

- Career
- Spirituality
- Personal Relationship
- Sex/Romance
- Children
- Family
- Exercise
- Friends
- Health/Diet
- Fun/Relaxation
- Ambitions/Business
- Travel
- Community
- Environment
- Other

Don't feel restricted by rules or deadlines. If you want to plan your wedding, your billion dollar payout, your retirement, or even your funeral that's your prerogative. This is your life you're creating, so create it how you want it to be, not how others think it should be. Once you start thinking concretely about what you want, you won't be able to help but get excited. Bit-by-bit, or maybe as a tidal wave, it will come to you. When it does, start writing (or talking, filming, cutting and pasting, etc.).

Here's your chance to write your own *I Have a Dream* speech. I have included a space below for you to write your own vision statement. For those who don't like to mark up books, go to my website, **www.gratitudeandgoals.com**. There you will find a free, downloadable *Gratitude and Goals* workbook.

When you create your vision, do it with joy, excitement and passion. If you can't get passionate about your own life, then what can you get passionate about? If you're concerned others will read your vision, then put it where it can't be found. But don't "edit" yourself because you're embarrassed what others might think.

My Vision Statement

_____

_____

_____

_____

_____

_____

_____

_____

_____

_____

_____

_____

_____

_____

_____

_____

_____

_____

_____

_____

_____

_____

_____

_____

_____

About twelve years ago, I created a vision board of the things I wanted for my future. But to tell you the truth, I don't even remember what was on it, let alone recall if any of it came true. Why? Because I didn't set goals to support my vision. It became nothing more to me than a piece of cardboard with a bunch of pictures on it. Once you create your vision, commit to moving in the direction of the images you choose by developing reachable goals to get you there.

All subsequent goals should in some way contribute towards the advancement of the vision you hold for the future. Of course you'll still need to do your daily tasks and to-do's. You may even have to work at a completely unrelated job, which you may not love, but nonetheless pays the bills. No matter what it is you're doing, always have a clear mental image of that "perfect" life you dream of, and get into the habit of continually setting new, _relevant_ goals to get you there. By doing so, you will naturally begin to ignore distractions and become more productive, creating a solid foundation for success.

Chapter Ten

LONG TERM AND SHORT TERM GOALS
How To Get From Where You Are To Where You Want To Be

"A strong passion for any object will ensure success, for the desire of the end will point out the means."

—WILLIAM HAZLITT—

Your level of success is determined by the strength of your vision. But daydreaming and positive thinking will only get you so far. The next step in the goal setting process is to break down your vision into individual long term goals to focus on, to guarantee your vision is served. Provided you have a robust vision statement, creating long term goals should be fairly easy.

Long term goals are the individual desires that make up your vision—the things you strive to obtain in the more distant future —the big house on the water, the foreign cars, the thriving business, the fit body, the loving marriage, the beautiful kids, perfect health, money in the bank, world travel and enough time on your hands to enjoy it all. Since long term goals are really just your vision statement broken down and sorted accordingly, we're not going to delve into the specifics of writing them here. The main focus of this book is on the more present day goals (short term goals, daily goals and action steps) that will help you accomplish your long term goals and, subsequently, your vision.

I can tell you, from my own experience, that there's a real danger to focusing too much attention on the future. Your long term goals can be a wonderful source of inspiration, but they can just as easily become a distraction from what really needs to be done today. When I first started to write this book, I would envision the big, beautiful house I would live in and the cars I would buy with all the money I was going to make. And yet I was still on my way to quitting another project. What was I doing wrong?

I was spending too much time fantasizing about the end results —how great my life was going to be *after* I finished the book— and not enough time planning my next steps (the process) to get the book done. For someone so inexperienced, the idea of writing a book, and then getting it sold, seemed like such a mammoth task. It was just easier to think positively about the end result rather than figure out how I was actually going to do it. That was before I figured out how to set short term goals . . .

Short Term Goals

Long term gain is simply the accumulation of your short term achievements. Long term goals are the motivation behind your desire to be successful, but the process of achieving them is very much driven by the small stuff—short term goals, daily goals and action steps. Even the slightest bit of progress is fundamental to success.

Long term goals are so far in the future, it's easy to get sidetracked, frustrated or confused. When this happens, we often lose enthusiasm and quit. Determining a short term goal will give you something in the present to work towards. It will kick-start you into action, build confidence and momentum, and keep you energized and so that you actually do more than just dream about your long term goals—you *achieve* them!

A life well lived is a life comprised of short term successes! A short term goal is something you aim to achieve at some point in the near future (in a few days, weeks or months). They have the power to turn any daydreamer into a doer by focusing your time, resources and attention on what needs to be done in the present. Your short term goals are your reason for waking up every day. They give you focus and help you gain a sense of accomplishment and ongoing progress.

Once you get into the habit, writing your short term goals should be one of the most exciting parts of your day. It gives you the opportunity to focus on your dreams and then come up with a plan to actualize them! Short term goals equal long term success. They are the plan of action to get you the money to buy that engagement ring, big house or new car. They are your means for fitting into the same size jeans you wore in high school. They are the strategy that will get you that "A" on your physics test and the support to help you quit smoking.

When writing your short term goals:

Be very specific.

Short term goals should be explicit and observable. E.g., "I want to lose twenty pounds by June first." vs. "I want to lose weight."

Make clear deadlines.

Don't stress about them, though. Deadlines should be flexible, unless of course the goal is something that actually has a deadline.

Create short term goals that are achievable.

They're meant to inspire, guide and motivate you, not overwhelm you. But always be true to your vision. Don't be afraid to go big. There is no such thing as a dream that's too big or too small.

Make them a priority.

Although some short term goals may be project based, such as finishing an assignment due at the end of the week, make sure you always have at least one short term goal that purely reflects your vision statement. Set your short term goals before your daily goals. Your daily goals should (in most cases) be a reflection of what needs to be done to accomplish your short term goals.

Be grateful in advance.

When writing them, get excited about the outcome, knowing you're creating it through your actions now.

Keep it simple.

Don't try to improve all areas of your life at the same time. That's like trying to quit smoking and lose fifteen pounds at the same time. If you set a goal and it seems a little daunting, rewrite it so it's easier to obtain. We all have our own pace and rhythm. Find yours and you'll do great.

The first short term goal I ever created was in direct response to my desire to write *Gratitude and Goals*. The whole idea of writing a book seemed far too intimidating since I had no previous experience as an author. The only way I was ever going to get it done was by breaking down my long term goal to complete the book into smaller, more easily attainable short term goals. I started by creating a short term goal to write for a total of seven hours in seven days (one hour each day for a week, estimated). Then I did the same thing the next week and then the next, etc.

Here are some short term goals from my own *Gratitude and Goals* Daily Journal . . .

My short term goals are:

1. To write for seven hours this week.
2. To speed-read every day for twenty-one consecutive days, in order to create a habit.
3. To complete the first draft of my book by December 1.

Every day when I sat down at my computer, I'd look up at the clock, and then jot down the time. I was honest about my efforts, keeping track of how much time I spent actually writing. If I got up to get coffee or answer the phone, I noted the time spent away from my goal. And when I was done for the day I marked down on a calendar just how much time I'd put in. Some days I did an hour or more, while on busier days I was lucky if I could string together half an hour. If the week was coming to an end and I was short of my goal, I would put in as much time as I had to in order to meet it. And I always did.

A short term goal is more than just a target, a maybe, or a someday type of thing. It's a commitment to you, your plans and vision. It's a concrete plan of action that requires your ongoing attention and nurturing. When you first begin, keep your first few short term goals small and very obtainable. This is a good way to help you get into the groove of writing and achieving them, without getting discouraged. Doing too much too fast will only overwhelm you!

With each success, major or minor, you will gain momentum toward achieving bigger and better goals. Your confidence will go up, and so will your faith in the power of goal setting, God and your own ability to work through any difficulties you may face along the way. As time goes on, you will build on this momentum by creating and achieving larger goals until you have achieved everything you've ever wanted.

Not sure where to start? Here are some areas in your life you may want to set goals for (or go to www.gratitudeandgoals. com for a free downloadable workbook):

Talents/Hobbies:

_____

_____

_____

_____

_____

_____

Financial:

_____

_____

_____

_____

_____

_____

Career:

_____

_____

_____

_____

_____

_____

Spiritual:

_____

_____

_____

_____

_____

Personal Relationship:

_____

_____

_____

_____

_____

Sex/Romance:

_____

_____

_____

_____

_____

Children:

_____
_____
_____
_____
_____
_____

Family:

_____
_____
_____
_____
_____
_____

Exercise:

_____
_____
_____
_____
_____
_____

Friends:

_____
_____
_____
_____
_____
_____

Health/Diet:

_____

_____

_____

_____

_____

Fun/Relaxation:

_____

_____

_____

_____

_____

Ambitions/Business:

_____

_____

_____

_____

_____

Travel:

_____

_____

_____

_____

_____

Community:

_____

_____

_____

_____

_____

_____

Environment:

_____

_____

_____

_____

_____

_____

Other:

_____

_____

_____

_____

_____

_____

Short term goals are not meant to be scary; they're meant to be exciting. They aren't meant to be difficult; they're meant to be obtainable. Don't feel you have to attack all areas of your list anytime soon. Focus first on the areas that are most important to you now or that will have the greatest overall impact on your life.

Even the most successful person was a beginner at some point. What do Oprah, Frank McCourt, Quincy Jones, Shania Twain, Andrew Carnegie, Bill Clinton, Larry Ellison, Napoleon Hill and Helen Keller all have in common? Humble beginnings! Every tiny effort put forth gradually contributed to their massive success.

When writing your first few short term goals, you'll also need to start humbly if you want to achieve massive success. Those who start out fast lose steam quickly, while those who take it slow and steady win the race.

When you get to the *Gratitude and Goals* Daily Journal section of this book, you'll notice that I've included two spaces for your short term goals. Don't feel the need to write two goals just because there are two spaces available. The best recipe for success is keeping it simple. Start with one goal, supporting it with sturdy daily goals and action steps. When your goal is met, come up with another short term goal to achieve something new. When you're comfortable with the process include another goal, slowly building momentum to bigger and better goals. It's also okay (when you're ready) to work on three, four, five or more short term goals, as long as they are manageable.

Establish Your Priorities

Twenty years from now, what do you think you'll regret most? Not putting in more hours at the office? Not spending more time driving everyone around to their games and practices? Not doing enough laundry? Your most valuable commodity is your time. Life is short and time is precious; neither should be wasted. Even on the busiest days, having a short term goal will help you set daily goals and prioritize your schedule so that you make time for what's really important: your dreams and goals.

Here's something to keep in mind. If you find when planning your day that you have no time left for yourself, flip your priority list upside down. Try working on your goals *first* and putting some of the other stuff second. Some days you may not get to respond to all incoming calls and e-mails. And guess what? The world won't end! Don't let the minutiae keep you from working toward the stuff that's really important. Yes, there will be days when you definitely have no time. And no matter how hard you try to juggle your schedule, other things will need to take precedence over your goals. That's life. But you can't expect things to change unless *you* take the action to change them. And that means giving them a reasonable degree of priority.

I read quite a few non-fiction books because I feel it's important to always be learning. In fact, I love personal development books so much, that I recently founded the Personal Development Book Club of America (find us at **www.pdbca.com**). When you learn, your mind expands, your confidence builds and you grow to become a better person in so many unexpected ways. One of my latest reads is *The 4-Hour Work Week* by Tim Ferriss. In it, Ferriss talks about Parkinson's

Law, which "dictates that a task will swell in (perceived) importance and complexity in relation to the time allotted for its completion." He continues, "If you haven't identified the mission-critical tasks and set aggressive start and end times for their completion, the unimportant becomes the important. Even if you know what's critical, without deadlines that create focus, the minor tasks forced upon you (or invented, in the case of the entrepreneur) will swell to consume time until another bit of minutiae jumps in to replace it, leaving you at the end of the day with nothing accomplished."

Your life is more than catering to the demands of others. Of course, giving of yourself is a vital part of life. But if you continue to make others' needs your number one priority, you may look back on your life one day as a dream unfulfilled. Sure, everyone around you will have benefited from your hard work and sacrifice, but will your soul feel a sense of fulfilled purpose?

❦

"Success depends on getting good at saying no without feeling guilty. You cannot get ahead with your own goals if you are always saying yes to someone else's projects. You can only get ahead with your desired lifestyle if you are focused on the things that will produce that lifestyle."

— JACK CANFIELD—

❦

Work, laundry and little Billy's soccer games are all important tasks, but not more important than your needs. Would you ever ask a friend to cancel an important business meeting so that he or she could hook up with you for coffee? Of course not! Would you ask your kids to miss a day of school just because you want to go to the mall instead of dropping them off? No way! Then why are your goals the first to be brushed aside when something else comes up? The time you set aside for your goals is just as important as a business meeting or a science project. If you don't make it so, then no one else will. Don't allow the needs of others get in the way of achieving your dreams. Your happiness and your future depend on you making your personal goals a priority. If you don't, who will?

Spouses, kids, bosses, friends, family, homework, charities, bill paying, phone calls and e-mail will find ways to take up your time if you let them. Once you establish the need to make time for yourself and your goals, others will see the positive effect it's having; not only on you but on them. They will begin to give you the time and space you need. Once you get over the initial anxiety (or guilt) of trying something new, you will begin to view this "me" time not as a luxury, but as a basic requirement for your survival.

So, where has all this talk of vision, long term and short term goals taken us? To a place where every day is a new beginning; where mistakes are corrected and dreams are realized . . .

CHAPTER ELEVEN

DAILY GOALS AND ACTION STEPS
How To Get Things Done

"A goal without a plan is just a wish."

—LARRY ELDER—

Let's do a quick recap. First we looked at the idea of having a *vision*. That's your richly textured dream for your future. It's your motivation behind wanting more, being more and having more. Next we discussed *long term goals;* the individual components that together make up your vision. Lastly we spoke of *short term goals;* the weekly/monthly/quarterly-type goals that let you build toward the attainment of your long term goals and ultimately your vision.

Short term goals define who we are, where we're headed and what we want in the present. We often talk about our goals as something we'd like to do "someday," when we have enough time, resources or money. When we do this, our goals become nothing more than empty dreams, stored away with the good china in the hope that we'll use them "someday." When is that someday going to be? Well, I'm here to tell you; that someday is today. Goals aren't something to be put off until the right time; they're something you CAN and WILL achieve today and every day by setting *daily goals* and *action steps*.

Daily Goals

"Our goals can only be reached through a vehicle of a plan, in which we must fervently believe, and upon which we must vigorously act. There is no other route to success."

—STEPHEN A. BRENNAN—

Your *Gratitude and Goals* Daily Journal is one of the best ways to get you on, and keep you on track to achieving your goals *every day*.

Repetition is the key to your success in any new habit you are trying to create. This is especially true when it comes to creating the habit of goal setting. Most other goal setting "gurus" will tell you that once you set your goals, it's best to *review* (reread and reevaluate) them every day, week or month. I've always found that instead of bringing me closer, merely reviewing them created a distance between me and my goals. I just didn't feel involved enough in the beginning to end *process*.

Simply rereading and reevaluating your goals is not enough. In order to stay completely involved in the process, it's best to write new goals *every day*, if possible. Writing down your goals takes only a few minutes, yet this step can make all the difference between success and failure. Having a written goal encourages you to prioritize and concentrate your efforts. It deepens your sense of connection and commitment to them, significantly increasing the probability of achievement.

A daily goal is a target you aim to achieve on the same day (or the following day) it is created. **But daily goals are much more than tasks on a to-do list . . .**

Daily goals are your day-to-day strategies for success.

No matter what you want to improve or achieve, setting one or two goals every day and fervently pursuing them, will help you attain your desire much faster and with more conviction, than if you did it only when the mood hit you. Even fifteen minutes dedicated to a goal is better than an hour spent daydreaming about it.

Daily goal setting is one of the most important things you can do for your success.

Unlike other goal setting methods which require that you only write new goals every few weeks or months, your *Gratitude and Goals* Daily Journal keeps your goals fresh in your mind by having you write them every day. Constantly writing and reevaluating your goals is the best way to engrain them in your brain. Because it's something you do every day, it keeps you constantly working and reworking your goals until they are achieved. Goal setting becomes a habit. Goal achievement becomes reality. Because it's an everyday thing, every day you are reminded to go after the things you want most in life, and you stay in goal achieving mode every day until they are yours.

Daily goals are the best way to increase your overall productivity.

Setting doable goals and sticking to them will get more done than you ever thought imaginable. A daily goal is more than just saying you're going to do something; it's a written commitment to actually doing it. If you stick to your commitment, you will vanquish procrastination and laziness from your life. Set one or two goals each day and COMPLETE THEM. Watch your stress diminish and your productivity skyrocket!

Daily goals keep you accountable to yourself.

You and only you are responsible for your life and the way you choose to live it. If you're not happy, BE the change you seek instead of looking to others to change things for you. When you set and achieve daily goals, you take responsibility for your life, but more importantly, you take control of your *destiny*.

Daily goals keep you from becoming overwhelmed.

Bit-by-bit, the *how* you will realize larger goals will reveal itself. And when they do, your new-found skill-set, based on your experience, will get you through them with confidence and ease.

Daily goals keep you focused on your larger goals.

A short term goal is the direction you want to head in and the daily goals are the required steps to get you there. They keep you actively pursuing your goals. Each day you complete your daily goals is another step closer to attaining your short term and eventually your long term goals.

Daily Goals vs. To-Do Lists

Life can get hectic. Sometimes even the simplest tasks, like making dinner or taking a shower, can burden your schedule. A simple to-do list can help manage your time and act as a reminder of all the practical things you want and need to do. However, it will do little to help you achieve your vision.

Daily goal setting is not intended to replace your to-do list, nor vice versa. In fact, the two should never be confused for one another. A to-do list is nothing more than a reminder of all the errands and responsibilities that require your attention. Your daily goals list is your "dream machine" and should command higher esteem.

If your daily to-do list is anything like mine, you probably have a dozen items on it that *should* be done that day. With all those tasks to think about, how is it possible to prioritize all of them? Goal setting prioritizes the one or two things each day that you are *determined* to achieve. Goals should never be lumped in with the laundry or a trip to the post office. Always keep goals separate from mundane tasks, to ensure they don't get lost in the shuffle.

On the other hand, daily tasks can and should become daily goals when need be. Allow me to explain. I'm a very on-the-go type of gal, who'd rather be outside in the fresh air with my kids than inside cooking and cleaning. I know there are a lot of people who like to do household chores, but to me, they've always seemed like a *necessary* waste of time! But that doesn't mean I'm unaware of the benefits of a clean home or a nutritious, home-cooked meal. It just means there are times when I need to make a conscious effort to do those things. This may mean setting a daily goal to help me get them done.

If doing the laundry or making dinner needs to be a top priority on some days, then certainly make it one of your daily goals. That way you can ensure that it will get done and you will reap the rewards from the victory when it is. That may sound contrary to what I stated about tasks and goals not being the same, but success comes in many ways.

Most days, my daily goals are written to complement my short term goals. For example, writing for an hour so that I can get closer to finishing my book, or drinking five glasses of water so I can help shed that extra ten pounds. But as I mentioned, sometimes I do use up one of my daily goals in order to complete a task if: a) it's important that it get done *today*, b) it will improve the quality of my or my family's life, c) it will aid in my personal growth, or d) it will weigh on my mind if I don't get it done. Having a nutritious dinner made on time for my family is something I really need to work on. It's about more than a meal; it's about my commitment to the health of my children. I feel better when I know what's in their food, and I feel lousy when it's the third time in a week we're grabbing take-out.

When I turn a task into a goal, I tackle it as a goal. I give it top priority. And when it's complete, I feel the same sense of satisfaction and accomplishment as I do with my other, "more important" goals.

Success Breeds Success

"Only put off until tomorrow what you are willing to die having left undone."

—PABLO PICASSO—

Goal setting and goal achieving are not skills you're born with. You learn them over time by trial and error, and a whole lot of persistence. Once you train yourself to be goal-oriented, you'll have programmed yourself to be success-oriented. Success breeds more success. No matter what your accomplishment, the success you gain in any one area of your life will inspire advancement in all the others.

Every day, when you write in your *Gratitude and Goals* Daily Journal, you are keeping your dreams alive. Give it a try. Start by setting one daily goal then see how you feel after you achieved it. I bet you'll feel pretty good about staying true to the commitment you made to yourself and will want to try it again. Once you have mastered achieving one or two daily goals, your confidence will go up and you'll feel substantially more empowered to go after your grander, short term and long term goals as well. Soon you will be able to set and accomplish several new goals each and every day.

Deciding to make something a priority is easier said than done, especially when there are so many other demands on your attention. Taking the time each morning to write down your goals will not only act as a reminder of a promise you've made to yourself, it will keep you committed to making it happen everyday. Without the constant reminder that daily goals provide, you may find yourself, as I did, spending your time on "time waster" activities like checking emails, reading the news, or doing chores; and never get anything "real" done. When you write daily goals and commit to them, things will get done; and you will be rewarded with certainty, knowing that YOU are in control of your life. YOU decide the direction it's heading in. YOU determine your success!

Action Steps

❧

"When it is obvious that the goals cannot be reached,
don't adjust the goals; adjust the action steps."

—CONFUCIUS—

❧

Here is where the winners are separated from the losers, and the successful rise above the pack. This is also where most people *fail* to achieve their goals. No matter who you are or what your situation; if you're a stay at home mother, a vice-president of a major corporation, a student, a first class athlete, a business owner, if you just lost your job, are financially or spiritually bankrupt, lonely or depressed . . . you will become a success story when you follow the principles outlined in this book. You'll become grateful, set goals and focus on them; *one action step at a time*. It's just that simple.

Do you have a job to find? A book to write? A soul mate to find? An exam to study for? A marathon to run? Taxes to file? Weight to lose? A wedding to plan? A closet to clean? A business to start? Goals to achieve? A dream to fulfill? Well, here's your chance to *finally* get it done!

Its okay to dream big, but you must be willing to start small. Remember, no large goal can ever be accomplished without the completion of smaller goals. Your vision of the future is achieved by accomplishing individual long term goals. Each long term goal can be achieved by setting and accomplishing many short term goals. And each short term goal can be achieved by setting and accomplishing daily goals. But how do daily goals get accomplished? Well, even they need a little help. You need to have a plan of action!

It's not enough to commit to writing your objectives for the day. A daily goal without structure is too vague. And with so much going on, even with the best intentions, your ambitions can easily be swept aside. If you want a guarantee that you will successfully complete each daily goal, you must get into the habit of working on them every day. You need to follow up each daily goal with a solid plan of action to see them through.

An action plan is a predetermined sequence of *action steps* required to see each goal through to completion. A thorough action plan takes out the guesswork of completing your goals by telling you *what* you need to do, *when* you need to do it, *how much* you need to do, *how long* you need to do it for, *where* it needs to be done and *with whom* you need to do it.

ALL daily goals are achievable by breaking them down into what I call *action steps*. In fact, no daily, short term or long term goal can ever be accomplished without them. **Action steps are the small, moment-to-moment, *simple* goals or tasks that need to be completed throughout your day, in order to achieve your daily goals:**

- They are the engine by which you achieve your daily goals.

- They are your *plan of action.*

- They are your commitment to *when, what, where* and *how* you plan to achieve your daily goals.

Action steps make everything simpler.

A good plan of action will keep you from becoming overwhelmed. It will focus your energy on what needs to be done *now* to accomplish your goals *today*.

Some daily goals may require several action steps to achieve, such as making two cold calls every hour throughout your business day, while others may only require one, like starting dinner at five o'clock, so that it hits the table at six. Either way, breaking down your daily goals into action steps will make getting it done easier and with more success than if you simply did it spontaneously. Structure is freedom. When you know exactly what you need to do and how you need to do it, you're free to live the rest of your day confident in the knowledge that you've done what is needed to accomplish your goals.

Action steps make your goals a priority.

Perhaps the most common reason people fail to achieve their daily goals is because they do not organize their day. They start their day with great intentions, then become busy and ultimately delay or forget about their goals altogether; putting them off for another day.

Prioritize your daily goals by creating specific action steps to achieve them. This way, your day becomes scheduled around your goals and the necessary action steps required to achieve them; prohibiting all other tasks and to-do's from taking over. Once you've written your action steps for each of your daily goals, you can then work through your day accordingly. If you know you're supposed to be at the gym at noon, you'll know better than to schedule a meeting at that time.

Action steps are the best hands-on approach to goal achieving.
From starting a business, to getting a raise, to finding the perfect partner, to losing weight; you must have a plan of action. That's what gets things done. Unlike a daily goal, which you write and then put aside, action steps keep you completely involved—without being overwhelmed or distracted—throughout the entire goal achieving process. A good plan of action will keep you so occupied in the habit of *doing* that any feelings of laziness or procrastination that attempt to creep in will quickly be overruled.

Even the most difficult challenge can be dealt with and the biggest goal can be completed if you have a plan of action. Knowing that your five year plan is to have a 10,000 square foot house is not enough. Knowing you want to lose ten pounds for your cousin's wedding in six weeks is not enough. Knowing that you want to make ten cold calls each day is not enough to get the job done. You must break down each goal into small, straightforward action steps to get you there. And as long as you complete *all* the steps required, you will without fail complete all of your goals.

A few months ago I started to gain a bit of weight and was becoming a bit discouraged about it. Then a friend of mine told me he actually lost weight just by drinking more water. That sounded like a great idea, especially since water is really good for you; regardless of the weight loss factor. So I decided I was going to try to lose weight by drinking more water. Since I don't like water, I knew the only way I would succeed would be by setting a daily goal.

I made a daily goal to drink five big glasses each day. In order to hit my five glass mark, I needed only to concentrate on my action steps: to drink one glass every two hours, starting at 9 a.m., 11 a.m., 1 p.m., 3 p.m., and 5 p.m. I increased my water intake substantially and was on my way to losing weight and improving my overall health.

How to Write Daily Goals and Action Steps

Writing your daily goals and action steps is one of the most productive things you can do each day. Daily goals will guide your day, but action steps will empower you with moment-to-moment control over your future. Goal setting shouldn't be a chore. In fact, it should be enlivening. (Hey, it's providing you the chance to create the life of your dreams here!) And once you get used to it, the whole process can be completed in less time than it takes to make breakfast. You can even do it *while* you eat breakfast!

Here are the steps I suggest you take when writing your daily goals and action steps in your *Gratitude and Goals* Daily Journal:

- Set your daily goals one at a time. It's best if you set them at the same time every day, in order to ingrain the habit of goal setting into your brain.

- Be concise and clear about both your daily goals and action steps. Make sure each one is manageable and attainable every step of the way. If for any reason you feel stressed after writing them, reevaluate and revise.

- Think of your daily goals as the important building blocks of your short and long term goals. In other words, your daily goals should be significant enough to advance you towards their completion. For example, if your short term goal is to lose twenty pounds, then one of your daily goals might be to hit the gym for an hour immediately after work. Your action steps might be to do a half hour on the stair climber and another half hour working on your lower body with weights.

• Write down one daily goal at a time, making sure to include the action steps before moving onto the next one.

Like all other steps in the goal setting process, action steps need to be planned ahead of time. They are not something you should be trying to figure out as you go along. After you set your goals in your *Gratitude and Goals* Daily Journal, immediately come up with a plan of action to achieve them. In other words, *what* you are going to achieve, followed up by *how* you are going to achieve it.

These are some actual daily goals and action steps I've set:

My daily goals are:

1. To drink five large glasses of water.
   Action steps: Drink a tall glass of water at 9 a.m., 11 a.m., 1 p.m., 3 p.m., and 5 p.m.

2. To write for one and a half hours.
   Action steps: Write while the baby is napping.

3. Make dinner.
   Action steps: Start cooking at 4 p.m.; serve at 5 p.m.

4. Workout for one hour.
   Action steps: Go to the gym from 3:30 p.m. to 4:30 p.m.

5. Read for thirty minutes.
   Action steps: Before going to bed.

Your action steps serve as a set of "how to" instructions to help you achieve your daily goals. When feelings of fear, doubt, or even laziness creep in, push them aside by refocusing on the action plan you've written in your *Gratitude and Goals* Daily Journal. Without hesitation, do the very next action step that's on the list. All that's left now is to do them . . . and voila, success!

Concentrate your efforts on the most immediate, smaller goals (action steps) as they come up. Sure, you can dream about the riches longer term goals will bring you in the future—that might be just the inspiration you need to keep going—but always balance dreaming with action here and now. Small targets equal small victories. Subtle as they are, small victories build on each other; getting you closer to where you want to be without all the stress of long term goals.

"Arriving at one point is the starting point to another."

—JOHN DEWEY—

What may seem like insignificant progress will add up to a larger achievement before you know it. Did you know you can read a 300 page book in five months by reading just two pages each day? (You can *write* a 300 page book by *writing* two pages a day, too. Six months from now you could be holding a bestseller in your hands!)

Anything you can think of can be accomplished if you simply break it down into small, manageable goals . . .

The method of goal setting I describe in this book pretty much goes for anything. You can lose weight and improve your health simply by increasing your water, fruit and vegetable intake each day. You can quit (or at least significantly decrease) smoking by lowering your cigarette consumption by one cigarette a day for thirty consecutive days. You can meet twelve potential life partners by talking to just three new people each week for a month. You can save over a thousand dollars by putting aside three bucks every day for a year. And even the most out of shape person can train for a marathon one lap around the track at a time.

Even something like cleaning a closet can turn into a lesson in confidence building if you let it. Instead of trying to tackle it all in one day, turn it into a one or two week job. Do sweaters one day, shoes the next, then handbags, etc. Or break it down into half hour daily sessions until it's clean. That's three and a half hours of progress in one week! With each successful phase (that's right, success even comes from cleaning a closet!), you will begin to feel less overwhelmed by the task and more confident in your abilities to get things accomplished.

With two small children around, our basement can easily look like a bomb hit it. When I ask my sons to clean it, they are, like most other children, less than enthusiastic. That's because all they can see is this massive chore they're being tortured into doing. When I break it down into categories, though, asking them to focus on just one thing at a time, like picking up the cars first, then the figurines and then the books; it becomes easier. And they're much more likely to complete it without complaint or frustration. In fact, when we turn it into a race, cleaning the basement can actually become fun.

Track Your Progress

Accomplishments written down in black and white inspire you to keep moving forward. But keeping track of your actual achievements and setbacks will keep you in constant check.

One thing I've found to be almost as important as writing out my goals, is keeping track of my progress. I kept track of my book writing progress by keeping track of how much time I spent typing on a calendar. That way I could look back at the number of hours I actually put in for the week. Missed hours were a signal to double my efforts before the week was up, in order to reach my goal. And I kept track of my water intake each day by making a small mark on my hand every time I drank a glass. On the days I forgot to mark down each glass, I didn't achieve my daily goal. In fact, there were days I entirely forgot about my goal to drink more water, just because I failed to keep track of my progress.

It doesn't matter *how* you choose to record it, but I strongly encourage you to keep track of every accomplishment and short-fall, making sure you're accountable for both. If your goal requires you to work for a certain amount of time, for example, write down the times you start and finish. Whether you use a journal, calendar, log or write on your hand, make a note of the duration/amount/progress. Tracking your input keeps your achievements (or lack thereof) right in front of your nose.

If you fall short of meeting a goal for some reason, make a note of it and see if you can somehow make up the difference. Knowing what you've done and what you need to do each day will determine your upcoming daily goals and action steps. Maybe your goal is to go to the gym five days a week. If on Friday you realize you only went three times instead of four, your weekend plans would need to include going to the gym both Saturday and Sunday, if you are to meet your goal.

In the last two years, because of *Gratitude and Goals*, I've been able to: start my own company, write four books (in various phases of development) and other projects, read dozens of books, take seminars, gain access to hundreds of new like-minded colleagues, friends, acquaintances and supporters, begin one-on-one coaching, do several speaking engagements, get into a regular workout schedule (I've lost several inches of fat and gained muscle), move into a beautiful house in a great neighborhood in California (this has always been my dream) and buy a new car, just to name a few.

Today, my husband is also a much happier, healthier, more spiritual, focused, determined, fearless and fulfilled person than he was when this all began. He has become more loving and at peace with the past and the mistakes he made. He regularly sets significant goals. He has started working out and eating well; resulting in an overall improvement in health, weight loss and strength. He has an incredible new job with the ability to make unlimited compensation. Plus, he works from home which has been an absolute blessing to our entire family. Not only does he help me achieve my goals by giving me much-needed time, but we have become a closer family as a result.

I have also become active at my son's school, become involved in more than one spiritual-based organization, have an incredible relationship with my kids, gained support from those interested in promoting me and my book, and now make elaborate dinners for my family on a regular basis . . . all thanks to this program! Most importantly, I've been able to succeed at *all* my projected short term goals, which inevitably get me closer to my long term goals and ultimately my vision.

"That which we persist in doing becomes easier,
not that the task itself has become easier,
but that our ability to perform it has improved."

—RALPH WALDO EMERSON—

Knowing your plans for *this moment* is just as important as knowing your vision for the future. Because this moment is really the only one you have; what you choose to do with it is what matters most. A moment wasted is a moment lost. When you set daily goals and attend to your plan of action right now, the future will take care of itself; one moment at a time.

Just try to remember; it's not a competition. Work at a pace that's right for *you*. Each small success will build upon the next, creating momentum. Before you know it, you'll have achieved the daily goals required to complete one short term goal and then another, and another, with each one getting you closer to your long term goals and vision.

You have within you *now* everything you need to create the life of your dreams. Be grateful for what you have inside and out. Persevere with faith and courage. Never allow the problems of tomorrow to stop you from achieving something today. They're just that—*tomorrow's* problems. Day-by-day, step-by-tiny step, you *can* and *will* make it happen. Focus on what needs to be accomplished today and you may be surprised to find that the problems of tomorrow and mistakes of yesterday have miraculously worked themselves out.

Chapter Twelve

WHY PEOPLE FAIL
How To Avoid The Pitfalls

"The greatest mistake a man can make
is to be afraid of making one."

—ELBERT HUBBARD—

Okay, let's say you've written a short term goal. Looks pretty good on paper, right? You start to fantasize about how great life will be once you've achieved it, but then all of a sudden you start to panic. *Am I ready? Am I capable? How will I achieve it?* Do you then come up with a list of reasons why you can't pursue it after all? Excuse after excuse comes at you with lightning speed . . . *I don't have enough time. I don't have enough money. I'm not old/ young enough. I'm not smart enough. I don't have the right education. I live too far away. My spouse won't let me. My kids won't let me. I don't know what I'm doing. It's too silly. It's too much work.*

Sound familiar?

We've all done it—created a goal, started a project or made a resolution, then failed, forgotten about it or given up the very next day, week or month. Let's face it. A good idea is only as good as its implementation. Excitement is where it all begins, but success doesn't come by being smarter or more passionate than the next guy. Patience, persistence and perseverance; those are the qualities of a winner.

No one is perfect. We have all failed at one thing or another; especially our goals. There is no *one* reason why we fail. **In fact, for every goal created there are at least a dozen ways to fail at it. Here are some of the biggies:**

1. Indecision

Can't decide what to do? Not sure what you like or want? Not sure what your talents and dreams are? Are you constantly changing your mind; jumping from one thing to another? Many of us fail because confusion keeps us from making a real commitment to our dreams. Confusion can lead to a pattern of starting and then giving up, or worse, doing nothing at all. If you can't decide what you want, how can you possibly achieve it?

Solution: If you haven't already done so, find a quiet place, grab a pen and do some serious soul searching. It's time to create the life you were meant to live! Each of us can access our own deepest wisdom, as well as the wisdom of God, if we only quiet down long enough and *listen. Listen?* What does it mean exactly, to *listen?* I found the answer to that question when I discovered gratitude.

Yes, the power of gratitude can even help you access the wisdom (or intuition) to help you uncover the answers you seek. As I mentioned before, I spent many years of my life asking God for things, including His guidance. In my prayers I would ask such questions as *What are my talents? What should I be doing with my life? What is my destiny?* When I stopped questioning and started giving thanks for my creativity, my intuition and all the other things I was good at and liked about myself. The answers came flooding to me . . . and I became wise enough to *listen* (to embrace the thoughts and feelings which arise, instead of fighting them). Within weeks I felt this amazing sense of calm. It was as if a huge weight was lifted from my shoulders. No longer did I feel the need to ask those questions or to fight my natural instincts.

To ask God for something is to assume you don't already have it. Asking questions such as *What should I do for a living? What are my talents? What should I be looking for in a partner? What do I like? What do I value?* is a huge waste of time. Whether you realize it or not, the answers are already inside of you. Instead, ask for *wisdom to recognize* the answer when they are shown to you. The answers are all around us; in our conversations, our prayers, on the TV, in books, at our workplace, our ceramics class, in church, at the gym and at school. They are everywhere, and they are inside us; in our head and in our heart. Or better yet, amplify your efforts by being grateful—because gratitude has a way of showing you what you already have—and in time and with practice, the wisdom will come.

"Always bear in mind that your own resolution to succeed is more important than any other one thing."

—ABRAHAM LINCOLN—

If you want to find the answers to some of life's "big" questions, look within first. I've provided some questions below which will help you reveal some of your truths, now, *in the present*. Read them over or write out your answers in the space provided. Take as long as you need. You don't have to answer all of them now, but at least read them, or, better yet, *ask* (or pray) for the wisdom to know the answers. And remember to *listen* for the answers. When you are prepared they will come!

This exercise can be used for just about anything, from figuring out what you want to do for a living, what you should take in college, to figuring out what you should be looking for in a partner. Be completely honest in your answers. By honesty I mean; what *you* think and feel, want and like, not what others would tell you to think, feel and want.

Start off by looking at your patterns; your ways of thinking, feeling and doing things. They hold the answers to many of your queries:

What kind of person are you? Are you ambitious? Are you always moving? Do you prefer to sit and relax? Are you a Type A personality who likes to be in control? Or do you just like to do the minimum amount of work required.

What are your true gifts and talents?

What comes naturally to you? Talking? Dancing? Selling? Drama? Business? Love? Helping people with their problems? Money? Real Estate?

What are you better at than everyone else?

What are your instincts? What do you intuitively know about yourself (and maybe even the world)?

What inspires you? What makes you happy?

What does your soul want and need? To sing? To create? To buy? To close large deals? To nurture? To serve? To teach? To build an empire?

What do you really like to do? Are they really your likes or are they someone else's interests imposed on you?

What things do you have a *sustained* passion for? Not just something you discovered a few days ago, but something you know you must have in your life.

What can't you live without?

What do you really dislike? Are you willing to bend a little on any of these?

What do you really want to do? Do you dream of running your own company one day, or do you prefer being an employee? Explore all possibilities.

If you could choose, what would be your work "uniform"? A T-shirt and jeans? A suit? A bathing suit? A lab coat? A director's hat?

What is your level of commitment? A lot? None? Neutral? Are you a committed type of person who sticks to one thing, or are you always looking for something new to fill a void?

What is your *vision* for the future? What do you want to have, to be, to do, to know in the next five to ten years?

What kind of person do you see yourself spending the rest of your life with? Someone who is loving, trustworthy, funny, outgoing, sensitive, athletic, caring and kind?

What do you really want to have within the next year or two? A house? A career? A spouse? Kids? To be a stay-at-home parent? To travel? To help people? To sit and relax every day? To build an empire?

What kind of people would you like to hang out with all day? What personality traits would they have?

How much money do you really want? When do you want it by? What do you want to do with it?

Where do you want to live? In a condo in the city? A small house in the suburbs? A mansion in Beverly Hills? A log house in the mountains? A hut on the beach? A secluded farm?

How do you want to furnish your surroundings?

How hard do you want to work? How do you see yourself getting to your workplace? With what kinds of people do you want to work? What hours do you want to put in? How much effort do you want to put in? What is your position? Owner? CEO? Support? Sales? Techie?

How can you best serve yourself and humanity? What is most natural for you?

Is there something you want so badly that you're willing to go to any lengths to get it?

How much do you value money, time to yourself, family, travel, learning, a challenge, creativity, security, power, fame, certainty, friendship, love, integrity, inspiration, responsibility, freedom, loyalty, etc.?

Is there one thing you would regret not doing before you die?

What is the one thing you MUST accomplish before you die?

What dream have you given up on that you wish you hadn't?

What are you most grateful for?

In the space provided (or in the free workbook provided on www.gratitudeandgoals.com), write down everything that comes to you. If you do this simple exercise day in and day out, you will soon begin to get a strong sense of who you are and what you really want and like.

_____

_____

_____

_____

_____

_____

_____

_____

_____

_____

_____

_____

_____

_____

_____

_____

_____

This list should <u>not</u> be influenced by:

- How much money you, your parents or your partner has

- Who you know or don't know

- Your experience or lack thereof

- Doing something (or being with someone) that you think can make you a lot of money. It's been proven that you can make a lot of money doing anything *the right way*.

- Doing something on a whim, or for a quick fix of excitement or money

- Other people

It is about *you*, and uncovering the things you know deep in your soul. It probably won't take more than a few days or weeks to gain substantial clarity. If it takes longer, don't worry. Once you've uncovered something, take a moment and be grateful for each discovery. And when you're done, make sure you give a heartfelt moment of thanks for the *wisdom* that you have been given to *know* them.

Answers may not come to you in the package you were expecting. We all know at least some of the things we are good at. And we have a good idea what some of our talents and gifts are, even if we can't seem to translate them into a way of making money. I can't sing or play an instrument, I'm not particularly athletic, and I'm terrible at math, geography and history. I do know what I am good at and what I do like. Combined, my interests and talents are incredibly strong and worthy of greatness. And so are yours.

This exercise may not tell you what exactly that you should be doing for a living or where you should look to find your soul mate. But your heart will speak to you, and if you clear away all the negative chitchat going on in your head and *really* listen, the missing pieces of the puzzle will be provided. Once you have some clarity, don't hesitate to create a vision statement for your future, and at least one short term goal, followed by relevant daily goals to get you started.

2. Making the Wrong Choice

You will not be motivated enough to succeed if you're going after something you don't truly want. Time after time, people take on jobs, relationships and responsibilities they're not really interested in in order to either satisfy the needs of others, fill a void, pay the bills or just get by. You cannot be truly happy doing something your soul does not desire.

Solution: Start by being completely honest with yourself. Refer to the last exercise. If you've already written a list of all the things your soul truly wants, then there should be no reason for you to be pursuing something else. Don't let what you don't know stop you from using what you do know. I don't know everything. And the longer I practice gratitude and continue to make conscious contact with my Higher Power, the more I become aware of that fact. But I do know what some of my talents and dreams are now, and I use them to the best of my abilities. As long as I listen and keep my eyes open to new opportunities, the answers continue to surface to my awareness every day.

Have the courage to follow your true desires; starting today. If it's not on the list, then don't do it. Remember, this is your life; you have to live with the consequences of your decisions. Do what's best for YOU.

3. Lack of Determination

If you're not committed to your goals, they will end up on the back burner or be totally forgotten. Failure tends to breed failure, just as success breeds success. Quitting in the face of temporary defeat, and starting and abandoning goals, creates a pattern of failure that can be challenging to overcome. If you're not willing to do whatever is needed to see your goals through from beginning to end, you're better off not setting them in the first place.

With all the opportunity in this world, you'd think that everyone would be a millionaire. But it's just not the case, is it? We all have dreams and goals. And while some are courageous enough to give them a go, only those who are willing to stick with it until they reach their goal will succeed.

Solution: If you're pursuing something that's important to you and you want to stay motivated, relentlessly pursue your short term goals. Remember, they're the ones that build up to your long term goals and ultimately your vision. Never allow yourself to get too overwhelmed or distracted. Work this program the way it is laid out, by first setting exciting short term and then daily goals; completing them one action step at a time. If you want something badly enough, never doubt it and never quit. Persevere until it's yours.

4. Lack of Concentration

One of the main reasons people don't obtain their goals is because they lack focus. If you've created goals in the past and failed, it may be because you got too busy doing other things or tried to do too much at once. If you're spreading yourself too thin, putting all your energy into chores, to-do's, work, etc., how do you expect to accomplish your own goals? There is only so much of you to go around. There's nothing wrong with being ambitious, but allowing yourself to get distracted can cause you to become stressed or overwhelmed. You simply can't achieve something if you don't make it a priority.

Solution: Make time. Allot a certain amount of time in your busy schedule to your daily goals. Stop spending all your time doing things for others, leaving nothing for yourself. The cooking, cleaning and job overtime will sometimes have to wait if they leave you too busy or too tired to work on your own life. You are here on this earth for only one reason. To achieve *your* destiny! Not to be Mandy's chauffeur, David's maid, or your boss's go-to guy. Those things may seem important to you now, but are they worth trading in your dreams for? Your dreams need tending!

To begin, concentrate on only one or two short term goals at a time, giving each your full attention until it is complete. Give yourself a half hour to an hour (more if possible) each day to work on your daily goals. And if you simply don't think there is enough time in the day, wake up a little bit earlier. It will be tough at first, but within a few weeks you will be used to it to the point where you will be able to do more. The results will be worth the effort!

Remember, these are *your* goals. Work on them at your own pace, but never give up or forget about them because you "don't have enough time." God gave you twenty-four hours in a day just like everyone else. At the end of your life, if you have not realized your dreams, you will surely conclude that the laundry could have waited!

5. The Feeling of Unworthiness

One of the greatest saboteurs of success is a deep-seated feeling of unworthiness. If, deep down, you don't think you're deserving of success, then no amount of goal setting will bring success to you. You will subconsciously push it away. We've all heard of lottery winners who were flat broke again three years later. They did not believe they deserved good fortune and so they repelled it when it came. If you want to have it all, first you have to know that *you deserve to have it all*. It's not up to anyone else to tell you what your worth or purpose is in life. Only you can decide that for yourself.

Solution: To root out your unworthy feelings and expunge them, you may need to do some honest inner reflection. Simply telling yourself your old belief isn't true won't cut it. Ultimately, you'll need to replace that flawed belief with a truer and more positive one. *You are loved by God and are fully deserving of all His blessings and abundance.* If it helps, tell yourself this message several times a day, with sincere gratitude and conviction.

If you want to have it all, first you have to believe you deserve to have it all. It's not up to another to tell you what your worth is in life. Only you can decide that for yourself. Today is a new day. Take control of your life today. The past is nothing more than a story for the history books. Now it's your turn to write the future as you wish. Create a vision statement and a powerful short term goals to work towards. Victories big and small will boost your confidence and give you more reason to be grateful. But whether you succeed or fail, is really up to you.

6. Fear

Fear is the number one reason why millions have never come close to achieving their dreams, and is a subject about which an entire library could be written. Fear is defined as a strong, unpleasant emotion (anxiety, apprehension) caused by anticipation of a potentially dangerous situation or event. In other words, it's all in our heads!

Fear is not tangible. It cannot *physically* harm you. Yet it's the worst of all enemies, since it's the core emotion that prompts all other self-defeating thoughts. Fear is what keeps us feeling "stuck" or "safe" in our current status. And for some, fear is the feeling which pushes them to take immediate action. We learn to avoid painful situations by attaching fear to things. Many believe fear is appropriate and necessary in order to avoid pain. After all, we ask how can a child learn not to stick her finger in an electric socket or avoid oncoming cars except through fear.

Some of the things we most commonly fear are that we're not capable or smart enough; we might look bad if we fail; we might be too cocky if we succeed.

What do you fear?

- Maybe you fear being too busy . . . or being bored.
- Maybe you fear being poor . . . or how life would change unpredictably if you were rich.
- Maybe you fear being alone . . . or committing to one person forever.
- Maybe you fear what kind of a parent you would make . . . or that you'll regret choosing not to have children at all.
- What about sex? Maybe you fear giving in too easily . . . or never being loved at all.

- Have you ever thought about owning your own company and then decided not to? Maybe you feared it might be too much responsibility . . . or, worse, having to work for someone else for the rest of your life.

If we attract what we focus on, then the more we focus on fear, the more dominant it becomes in our lives. Fear of being hurt by the unknown; the "*how* to achieve it," the "what ifs" and even the outcome, is what often prevents us from pursuing our dreams. We lie to ourselves and others, saying we're satisfied with what we have, when really we're not. We think we're letting ourselves off the hook. That way we never have to risk discomfort or failure. But we also never have to risk success.

If you let it, this one little word, "fear," will steal your dreams and your life. It will leave you feeling empty and unfulfilled, and it will keep you from ever becoming all that you can be.

Fear is the reason we so often choose to do nothing. To live a life without risk is considerably safer, but is it satisfying? What do you think would happen if you *faced* your fears and tried stepping outside the box? Would doing so hurt or endanger yourself or another? If the answer is, "no," then what do you really have to lose? On the other hand, what might you gain by "owning" your fears and going for the gold? Fulfillment, wealth, independence, love, freedom, health, and joy; perhaps?

Solution: Face your fear. The world was built by those who faced their fears and exceeded them!

Stop judging your fear. It is neither good nor bad. It just *is*. Instead, be grateful to the feeling you label "fear." In the face of gratitude, that fear will transform into courage and you will feel empowered to move beyond it. Accomplishing any goal requires courage, and what is courage without fear? Nothing; it doesn't exist. If need be, call upon God's help to access the courage inside you. Whether you know it or not, courage, like God, is always with you, waiting for you to call upon it.

Attack all feelings of fear head-on by taking immediate and constant action. Set a goal and be determined to achieve it. If it feels uncomfortable at first, push even harder. When it's all over, and let me assure you that it will be, you will be wiser, stronger and more confident and successful than before.

7. Procrastination

Putting something off until later—*procrastination*—is one of the most common and most preventable causes of failure. But what causes us to procrastinate? Our conditions aren't quite right? There's not enough time? It's just not the "right" time? You work best under pressure? Or, if we were to be totally honest, do we really procrastinate because of feelings of inconvenience, discomfort, laziness or even fear? What are these really but excuses for avoiding potential pain?

Solution: There is no such thing as the perfect time, the perfect condition or the right amount of experience or resources needed to start something. The best time is now, and the perfect conditions are right here with what you have to work with. You don't need a million dollars to start your business, you don't need a computer to write your screenplay, you don't have to be a certain weight to go on a date, you don't need the right music in your iPod to go for a jog and you don't need the whole day to yourself in order to do research or make cold calls. What you need is to stop making excuses and start taking action now!

Projects and tasks are rarely cumbersome and scary at the outset. They become that way the longer we put them off. Using the example mentioned in the last chapter, a messy, over-packed closet is really nothing more than that—a messy, over-packed closet. However, just the thought of cleaning it can cause you to feel weighed down, stressed, and guilt ridden if it's not dealt with right away. So much stress over a closet?

More often than not, the tasks and projects which await us are in actuality much smaller than we make them out to be. The longer we wait, the more blown out of proportion they become, and the more convinced we become that they can never be accomplished without a huge amount of suffering. As a result, the likelihood that it will never be completed increases. But in reality, it's not the project itself, but the waiting, the putting off, and the feelings that follow which cause us to feel this way.

Recently, I was faced with having to fill out some paperwork in order to get my son into preschool for the fall. It needed to be done right away since the spaces were filing up fast. And yet I put it off, for no other reason than the fact that I absolutely hate doing paperwork. In fact, I waited so long the year before that my son didn't get in. So, after weeks of waiting, and dreading, and stressing and feeling burdened, while at the same time guilty, I finally decided to download the forms and get started. I was shocked to find out there was only one form, with only a few lines. That was it! In fact, I felt far more stress just thinking about having to do it than actually doing it. If only I had used some of that time actually looking into it rather than trying to avoid it, and of course stress about it, I would have known. And to think that I almost made the same mistake I made last year because I procrastinated!

Nothing breaks the pattern of procrastination like good habits. But good habits don't just magically occur; you have to create them by setting goals and making plans. Even the smallest bit of progress can effectively break the procrastination cycle and shrink the magnitude of the task to a more realistic size. As you begin to make steady progress, you will be reinforcing positive work habits, as well as building your self-confidence. The next steps toward completion will be easier to begin, and inevitably accomplish, once you get over the initial hump.

"The only way around is through."

—ROBERT FROST—

Are you one of those people who procrastinate because you've convinced yourself you don't have enough time? We've learned a lot in the last few chapters about breaking down goals. Things don't have to be completed all at once. Every goal, no matter how large, can be broken down into smaller, more achievable goals and action steps. Let's say, for example, that you only have six days left to get your taxes done. Predict how long you think it's going to take you to finish, and then divide that by how much time you have left. If your deadline is in six days and you think it will take four hours to complete, then plan to work on them for just forty minutes each evening for the next six days.

Overcome procrastination by replacing bad work habits and excuses with good work habits and action. Stop wasting time worrying about what you think are your limitations. Instead, create a vision in your head of what you want the final outcome to look like. Don't worry that it may not turn out exactly as you anticipated. It may turn out even better! Then set a specific goal to get it done by.

Stop getting ready. Stop procrastinating. There is no such thing as just the right condition or timing. Right now, where you are, with what you have and what you know already—that is the right condition. Then, whether you think you're ready or not, start by taking immediate action, with the knowledge, time and resources you do have. Continue to create definite action steps to keep the momentum going. Everything else will fall into place as they're needed most.

Here are a few more reasons people fail to begin or achieve their goals:

- It will take too much time to develop.
- It will take too long to achieve.
- A skill set is lacking.
- There is a shortage of ideas.
- There is a perceived risk of failure.
- There is poor idea selection.
- They don't feel successful in their endeavor.
- They don't know how to "buy in."

With each goal achieved, another fear is squashed. Having a daily goal to work towards will limit your fear about the future. Direct your attention towards one day or even one thing at a time and fear won't get a foothold. You will be too busy working on the requirements of today to worry about the future. I'm not suggesting you shouldn't take precautions to avoid future problems, but by being more effective today, you will dramatically decrease the potential for problems tomorrow.

Who Is in Control of Your Destiny Anyway?

Are you the master of your destiny? If not, then who is? As it turns out, the more in-control you feel of your destiny, the higher your self-confidence will be. Those who feel they're the creators of their fate accept personal responsibility for all that happens to them—*good or bad*. They confidently take action and make decisions; careful not to blame others for the outcome. And when they do experience failure, they come up with a new approach and get right back on the horse and try again. They never give up on goals because that would mean giving up on themselves.

Unfortunately, most people renounce control of their lives; giving away their power to outside forces. They become pawns in their own lives, always *reacting* to situations; never creating them.

You are a magnificent and deeply worthy person. You are God's child! You were born with unique qualities and talents that are begging to be maximized. Have absolute confidence that you can do anything you desire; set goals and pursue them relentlessly; knowing God is cheering you on all the way.

You were born into this world feeling unstoppable, but over time you were reprogrammed to think less of yourself. Know this: life is ultimately harder for those who get pushed around in this world than for those who take command of it. NOW is your time to take back the power that is your birthright.

CHAPTER THIRTEEN

BUILDING THE
CONFIDENCE MUSCLE

"We need to internalize this idea of excellence.
Not many folks spend a lot of time trying to be excellent."

—BARACK OBAMA—

Successful people are confident people. Just ask anyone who's living the life you dream of. But how do you act confidently if you think you have little or no confidence to begin with?

Confidence is a belief in yourself and a feeling of self-assurance that you *can* get something done. First, let me start by saying that you do have confidence, whether you realize it or not. Think of all of the things you've done in your life so far: learning to walk, dance, talk, sing, read, ride a bike, drive a car, etc. Maybe you graduated from high school or college, got married, had children, got into or out of a relationship, quit an unwanted habit, or learned a new habit, a new hobby, a new recipe, a new language, etc. Think of all the things you may have learned about yourself already by reading and working through the program in this book! You needed to overcome procrastination and have a certain amount of initiative to do that. Give yourself some credit!

I have two sons—three years old, and fourteen months old. Every day I get the privilege of watching them learn the complex tasks we grown-ups take for granted. The other day my baby took his first step. That's absolutely huge for him, because he didn't just wake up one morning and start walking. It took months of grabbing onto things and falling down before he confidently took a step on his own. The same goes for my other son, who is learning to read and write. It's very exciting to see him form simple two letter words.

These are astonishingly complex tasks, requiring intelligence and coordination that would boggle the most powerful computer on the planet, and yet I don't think I've ever met anyone who has actually given themselves credit for learning them. As adults, we've known how to do them for so long we can't even remember learning them. But watching children learn, you see they are not innately fearless. They *want* to have and do more. They *want* to grow, learn and to accomplish new tasks; just like adults.

There must have been a time when you didn't let doubt rule you or you'd still be sitting on your mother's lap, waiting for her to feed you. That sounds ridiculous, right? Of course it does, and yet when I remind people about the confidence they displayed as a child, most say that children are just naturally fearless because they don't know any better. I am here to tell you they are not. They are risk-takers, and so were you once!

The difference between them and us is that they have much bigger comfort zones than we do. We are born into this world open to endless ideas and possibilities. The longer we are here on this earth, the more set in our ways we become and the more difficult we find it to step outside of ourselves to try something new.

When trying something new, the first step is always the hardest, because it's the one which takes us out of our comfort zone. But we cannot change unless we step outside of the safe zone and confront our fear. Each time we try (or learn) something new we expand our parameters. And the more we push ourselves in new ways, the more flexible we will become. Not only will we gain the ability to cope with change, but also the courage to seek out new opportunities to create it.

Like courage, confidence is not the absence of fear, but what you become by overcoming it. Fear is natural. Show me a man who says he fears nothing and I'll show you someone who's full of you-know-what! Fear is innate. It's what keeps our survival skills strong and our instincts sharp. It's our job to move beyond our comfort zones if we're to achieve any sort of success in our life. By defeating our fears one at a time, we become less concerned by the little things life throws our way, freeing us to move on to bigger goals and dreams.

❧

Fear never completely goes away. It's what we make of it, learn from it, and do with it which makes us who we are today and is the determining factor of our tomorrow.

❧

People all too often make excuses for why they can't succeed: my mother abandoned me when I was a child, my parents were alcoholics, my father hit me, I was molested, we were poor, I didn't finish school, etc. Blame is nothing more than the refusal to take responsibility for our own lives. Whether you admit it or not, you're a grown up now, and ONLY YOU are responsible for your life. It's impossible to achieve your dreams if you continue to make excuses, or blame others for your problems and shortcomings. No matter how "justified" your anger is at someone else, only *you* are responsible for limiting your future by hanging onto the past.

If you have no confidence because you believe you've had a disadvantaged life, then it's time to take a good hard look in the mirror. If what you see is someone who is beaten down by all the "heavy lifting" you've had to do, look again. I may not know everything there is to know about physiology, but I do know this; when humans continually lift heavy objects their bodies get stronger, not weaker. I've never met a weak weightlifter. Our minds are like our bodies. The more we "lift," the stronger and more capable we get.

Every day you're caught up in the past is a day wasted. What kind of legacy do you want to leave; one of blame and regret, or one of love, happiness and success? It's entirely up to you!

***

"Life is not lost by dying; life is lost minute by minute, day by dragging day, in all the thousand small uncaring ways."

—STEPHEN VINCENT BENET—

***

When you feel resistant to doing something, carefully explore what is causing you to feel that way. Is it fear that's tricking you into believing you're not capable or worthy? If you want to build confidence, then do the *opposite* of what your fears are telling you (as long as it won't endanger you or someone else, of course). Make a *decision* to do it, *visualize a positive outcome*, and act on it; knowing you have nothing to lose and, quite possibly, something great to gain. Take it one step at a time, setting small, daily goals until it is accomplished.

Build the confidence muscle by attacking your fears head on!

Triumph over them by having an open mind, and the courage to seek out and act upon new ideas and opportunities. Every time you try something new, you're filling your brain with knowledge. Knowledge is power! The more you know, the more confident you will be. Have you ever met someone at the top of their game who lacked confidence?

No one gets ahead on talent alone. Even the most gifted person needs to overcome obstacles. Is Tiger Woods afraid to make a shot with millions of people watching? Is Oprah afraid to interview the President? Is Donald Trump scared to build skyscrapers? Does Bill Gates worry that no one will buy the newest version of Windows? I'm sure all these people *were* afraid at one time. But with practice, they've gained the unshakable confidence to become the best at what they do.

Absolute confidence doesn't happen overnight. It's a muscle that grows and is nurtured over time through self-love, faith and the success you achieve from taking chances. What are you good at? Playing the piano? Basketball? Exercising? Helping others, cooking, maybe even sex? How do you feel when you do those things? Unstoppable? Energized? Accomplished? Capable? Powerful? When you allow yourself to feel accomplished (confident) in one area, you're more likely to take chances in others. Small goals may reap small rewards, but each victory builds your self-esteem and overall confidence. Harnessing those feelings of success will motivate you to try bigger and better things.

My life has been filled with its share of ups and downs. There have been some wonderful moments that showed me what I wanted most out of life. But it was during the worst of times that I learned the most about how to attract them. It was during the worst relationships that I decided I was worth better. It was during the worst jobs that I decided to stop wasting my time and be true to my talents and goals. It was when my health was at its worst that I decided to make drastic changes to become healthier. And it was during the worst financial struggles that I became responsible for my life; motivating me into action—to do with it what I've always dreamed of.

We work our whole lives trying to have and be the things we dream of. But we gain the most from the adversities we face on the journey. It's through climbing out of life's holes that we develop confidence in our resilience, our strength and our ingenuity! Dr. Michael Bernard Beckwith, visionary, and one of the masters of *The Secret* is quoted as saying, *"I believe that you're great; that there's something magnificent about you. Regardless of what has happened to you in your life, regardless of how young or how old you think you might be, the moment you begin to think properly, this something that is within you, this power within you that's greater than the world, it will begin to emerge. It will take over your life. It will feed you, it will clothe you, it will guide you, protect you, direct you, sustain your very existence. If you let it! Now that is what I know, for sure."*

The most powerful statement you can make about yourself is "I am." It indicates the confidence you have in yourself to "be" what you say you are and to manifest what you desire. The word "want," as in "I want to be wealthy" or "I want to be successful," indicates that there's something lacking in the present moment. Remember, that for as long as you have God in your heart and you have faith, you have no reason to feel as though you "lack" anything. You already possess everything that you will ever need to succeed. And the moment you decide it to be so, it will be.

People who make "I am" statements halfheartedly do so because they think they're lying to themselves. "How can I honestly say, 'I'm wealthy,' when it's obvious that I'm not?" they ask. You must remind yourself that the Universe responds to the frequency you set. When you emphasize what you want (the lack, the absence of), rather than what you *have*, you create more of the same—the *state of wanting*. When you emphasize the "I am," that too becomes your reality; whether it is positive—or *negative* ("I have no time," for example).

It's important to reprogram yourself to "be" whatever it is that you desire. Instead of saying, "I want to be happy," tell yourself, "I am happy." Say it throughout the day, if necessary. Start by being grateful for all the things which bring you happiness. "I am" statements are a great way of telling the Universe your intentions. By doing this often, you reprogram your way of thinking to accept these words as fact—that you *are* happy, rather than *waiting* to be happy. And then act accordingly.

Gratitude Creates Confidence

It's difficult to motivate yourself to try something new when you simply don't have confidence in your abilities to do it. This happens when you focus too much on what you don't have (money, time, etc.) and not on what you do have. How do we find this confidence? Gratitude, of course!

Gratitude keeps us focused on our strengths, not our failings. Remember the prayer, *"For all that I am and all that I have, I am grateful. I have no complaints."* It's a reminder that you have everything you need inside you to "be" the change you seek. If you seek happiness, know that it's in you waiting to be called upon. If you want money, tap into that part of you which recognizes the abundance around and within you. If you are lost or confused, ask your Higher Power for the wisdom to know His guidance.

Appreciation for what you already have, along with an understanding that God is guiding you forward, can give you confidence to tackle any kind of goal. It's what you do with that motivation which matters most. You can start to feel confident right now by practicing gratitude. Sit down and list all your strengths and talents if this helps. Acknowledge each one with a heartfelt surge of thanks for each. Understand the benefits of what you already possess instead of dwelling on personal weaknesses and past failures.

Take the 21 Day Challenge

There will always be a certain level of discomfort in anything new you try. That doesn't mean it's wrong, or even wrong for you. Habits are created through sustained effort, practice and perseverance. Sustained effort keeps the momentum going. Practice will cast aside any uncomfortable feelings the new activity gives you. Perseverance will turn it into a habit. As self-evident as this may sound, you will only be uncomfortable until you become comfortable. Once the new activity becomes habit, you'll start to see the difference it's making in your life and you'll never want to go back to the way your life was without it.

Dr. Maxwell Maltz, creator of the "21 day habit" theory, states that it takes approximately twenty-one consecutive days of practice for a new habit, thought or routine to become ingrained into memory. If you want to create a new habit and make it stick, it will take about three weeks of practice before your brain will accept the new habit as the norm. Once the twenty-one days are up, it will be almost second nature to keep the momentum going. The whole point of developing a new habit is to keep up with it, and not give it up. The likelihood of its becoming a permanent part of your daily routine increases the longer you stick with it past the twenty-one day mark. And of course, the more you enjoy what you're doing, the easier it will become and the better you will become at doing it.

Stopping and starting projects can rob you of accomplishing anything worthwhile. What's the point of creating a new habit if you stop doing it after twenty-one days is up? The *Gratitude and Goals* Daily Journal is not just another thing to make your life more demanding. My intention when originally designing it for myself was to simplify my life, by prioritizing my day more efficiently. If you stick with it, it can and will help you forge good habits that last a lifetime.

This is a very forgiving program. If you find yourself a bit off track or miss a day of writing in your journal, don't beat yourself up. Just dive back in without further delay. Even if you stop and start twenty times in twenty different ways, that's okay. You just might need *twenty-one* times to get it right! In fact, some of the greatest inventions of our time owe their existence to persistence and perseverance. After five years and 5,127 prototypes, the Dyson G-Force bagless vacuum cleaner was created. It took Edison over 10,000 "failed" attempts before he invented the light bulb. And the creator of the Head skis broke thousands of prototypes and was booed off the slopes before he made his millions.

Before deciding this program isn't for you, give it a try! Don't just throw it on the shelf with all the other dust collectors. I challenge you to create a habit of submitting an entry in your *Gratitude and Goals* Daily Journal for twenty-one consecutive days. Keep honest and accurate track of your progress. Wait and see what happens! When you've reached twenty-one consecutive days, look back at the results. How do you feel? What positive changes have you made? What have you learned about yourself from this experience? What goals have you achieved? Was it worth it? What's next on your list to achieve?

I guarantee that you will receive amazing results after only twenty-one days *or less* of working this program. And if you are not completely satisfied, for whatever reason, please send this book back to the store (or wherever you bought it) for a full, money-back refund. No strings attached!

What do you have to lose (except the chains that are keeping your dreams in bondage)?

Chapter Fourteen

THE MOST IMPORTANT RELATIONSHIP YOU CAN HAVE IS WITH YOURSELF

"You may not have been responsible for your heritage,
but you are responsible for your future."

—AUTHOR UNKNOWN—

So far we've discussed how to achieve your external goals. Now we will focus on your inner world; how you manage your thoughts, your feelings and your behavior.

Despite all the pressure to keep up with the Joneses, your happiness really has very little to do with what you do or don't have. Nor does it have anything to do with your education, where you live, or your upbringing. It *is* a direct result, however, of *who you are today*—what you think and believe, what you feel, how you behave and most importantly, how much you *enjoy* your life. Your outside world is merely a reflection of your inside world— "as within, so without." So it makes sense that in order to receive positive benefits in your outside world, you must be willing to create positive changes on the inside.

"We don't see things as they are; we see them as we are."

—ANAIS NIN—

Let's think back to the beginning of the book, when we discussed *thought*. Our thoughts, or, more importantly, how we manage them, influence our feelings and the way we behave, determine "who" we are today. Nothing in life—no action, no word, no thought, and no situation, *nothing* has any meaning until we give it a meaning. Our thoughts, feelings and perceptions fill in the blanks of what would otherwise be empty space. We can go through life putting our own slant on pretty much everything and everyone we meet. We even do it to ourselves. Things are as we *believe* them to be. People are as we *believe* them to be. We are as we *believe* ourselves to be.

Who we are is ever evolving—or at least it *should* be. The old saying, "a leopard can't change his spots," is rubbish. Of course we can't change the color of our skin any more than a leopard can change its spots. But that doesn't mean we have to remain stagnant. We can change our habits and improve our overall happiness, as soon as we make a conscious *decision* to do so.

You're happiest when you're on a path of personal development. It's not just about what you can buy or what car you drive. Personal development is about *becoming;* reaching new levels of awareness through knowledge and experience. It's about getting to a point where you intuitively know what you like and don't like. It is about knowing *how* to be good and realizing what changes you need to make to free yourself from self-destructive thoughts, feelings and behaviors. Get to know yourself by looking at your thoughts and beliefs, understanding how they influence your way of being. You cannot alter reality, but you can change the way you *feel* about it. Be consciously aware of the *way* you think—not only *what* you think about, but the effect your thoughts have on your life today.

"The truth will set you free. But before it does,
it might make you angry."

—JERRY JOINER—

Consider the relationship you have with yourself like an undivorceable marriage. No matter where you go, or how hard you try, you're stuck with *you;* for better or for worse. You can run, but the one person you can't hide from is yourself. You can end relationships with others, quit your job, even try the geographical cure and move away. The painful fact is that people are the same wherever you go, and so are you! No matter how hard you try to escape, you'll still be stuck with your defeatist ways. Until you do the work to change.

As humans, we're meant to progress by becoming physically, emotionally, intellectually *and* spiritually stronger. When we strive to improve ourselves, we flourish. It's when we cease to strive that we begin to wither. **Personal growth involves more than just changing careers, falling in love or getting in shape. It is an ongoing awareness to:**

- Be more loving, patient and kind
- Accept that whatever is, *is*
- Give without expecting anything in return
- Really *listen* and be more empathetic to others
- Be self-compassionate
- Live your highest truth; do what you were meant to
- Love fully and without reservation
- Live honestly and purely
- Be more at peace with yourself
- Trust in the love of God
- Believe in your own worth and dignity

These universal lessons can take a lifetime to master, but the rewards are immeasurable. It doesn't matter who you were five years or five minutes ago. What is important is to know who you *intend* to be from this point forward, and *become* that person.

The Four A's of Personal Development

There are over six billion people in the world, each with their own agenda. With that many people trying to exercise personal control, there will inevitably be some turbulence. But what do you suppose would happen if everyone worked at being their very best selves? Wouldn't this world be a better place to live? Wouldn't *your* world be a better place? If what you want is to change the world, you need first to change *yourself.* How do we do that? Focus on what I call . . .

The Four A's of Personal Development:

1. Awareness

2. Acceptance

3. Accountability

4. Action

Awareness

Awareness is simply admitting there is a problem; that your life is not as you want it to be.

Ignorance is bliss, but not when it's keeping you emotionally, spiritually and financially broke! Denial is a strange thing. It only works for us as long as things are going smoothly. It is the approach we use to pretend we're okay as we are and don't need to change. Eventually reality catches up and we're forced to make a decision: to live a lie and slowly lose ourselves, or take action and *become* the person we're meant to be.

You can't expect to improve *anything* unless you're aware that there's a need for improvement. And that's the problem, isn't it? Many times we don't even realize there's something that needs changing. We tell ourselves everything's fine because to admit the problem would mean we'd have to do the work to fix it. So we tell ourselves, "That's just the way life is."

Awareness is the key to any sort of change. Instead of pretending it's all good, open your eyes and acknowledge what's happening. Are you living your highest truth? Are you feeling one way but convincing yourself you feel another? Do you like one thing while allowing others to believe you like another? Are you smiling on the outside but secretly torn apart on the inside? Are you angry, frustrated or confused, but all the while keeping up appearances?

Be honest with yourself about what's really going on inside you. This is the first step towards the personal growth you desire. The power of honesty is amazing. Many people tend to look at honesty as though it were one of the Ten Commandments—as something only pure and righteous people practice. Honesty is for everyone, all the time. It is the high road to inner peace and happiness. Honesty is about being truthful to the world, but, more importantly, it is about being truthful to you; facing yourself, your life and the troubling things (your faults and insecurities) you've been trying to ignore.

Becoming aware there is a need for change can sometimes be the most difficult part of all. Initially, when you become aware of a shortcoming, make a conscious effort to tell yourself you must remove it from your life. Your increased awareness of this shortcoming will automatically cause a shift to occur, paving the way for you to change. Let's say you realize you haven't been the best listener and would like to become better. You become aware of the fact that every time another person is talking you are quick to interrupt them. The next time you are in a conversation and interrupt, mentally forgive yourself and then allow the conversation to revert back to them. Or better yet, become aware of the signs and catch yourself *before* it happens!

Guilt and Shame

Many of us are embarrassed to admit that we really want something big and bold; that we want to become rich, famous, or wildly successful. Maybe we fear that being or having more than the next guy will mean we'll be criticized or made to feel immoral. Maybe we just don't feel worthy of good things, or ashamed because "Godly people" aren't supposed to want these types of material things. Instead of being true to our dreams and desires, we choose to feel guilty about them, and so we go through life doing what we assume others think we *should* do.

There's so much scrutiny in the world that the simple thought of being successful can be scary. Most people would take a million dollars if offered it, and yet the very same people go out of their way to disapprove of others who have more than them, and some even try to make them feel guilty for their good fortune.

I've felt this kind of pressure all my life. I've always been a big dreamer. By big, I mean crazy big! Just the other day I mentioned to one of my new friends that I wanted to have a full-time maid, a personal assistant, a nanny and a personal chef. She laughed. I could tell she was laughing because she thought I was just joking. I wasn't.

I guess the lesson here is to be careful about who you tell your dreams to. Your dream is not a joke, nor is it something to be ashamed of. It just means you are telling it to the wrong people. Tell people who will take it seriously. Better yet, tell a successful person. They'll support you!

⸻

Money is a means to an end. Not the end itself.

⸻

Money is not bad. It's unprejudiced. Those who do bad things with it are bad. Money can be used to do good things. It can enrich your life and the lives of others by creating opportunity. Money can give you the power to change the world in ways that lack of money cannot. There are many people with a lot of money who are in fact very generous with their good fortune. Look at all the wonderful things Bill and Melinda Gates have been able to do through their charity foundation, for example.

Being totally honest about who you are and what you want is the best thing you can ever do for yourself. Studies show that eccentrics are in fact much happier and healthier than most. Since their only goal in life is to be honest with themselves, they see no need to please people. Instead of trying to live up to the expectations of others, they do what makes them happy, without pressure, shame or guilt. And since they don't put their bodies through the stress that pretending (lying) so often reaps, their immune systems are stronger and they live longer, healthier and happier lives than most others.

Admitting you want more money (success, higher education, passion, a better house, an expensive car, a perfect body, a closer relationship with God, etc.) may require a leap of courage. It is certainly nothing to be ashamed of. The world desperately needs your ideas and input. It needs you to go after your dreams. Some of the most successful people in the world are where they are today because they overcame adversity. Stop feeling conflicted about wanting more. Regardless of what others say, it's okay to want good things—*it really is.*

People don't have to accept or even understand your dreams and desires. At the same time, you must stop judging others for what they have. You cannot simultaneously condemn something and desire it. This sets up an inner conflict that prevents your desires from coming to you. The Universal Law of Non-Resistance states that that which you resist, persists. And the more you resist, the greater its effect on your life. In other words, if we want to be happier, more confident and in tune with our own lives and dreams, we must begin to let go and just *accept.*

Which leads us to . . .

Acceptance

Acceptance is the key to your peace of mind. It means living without expectation, judgment or criticism. It means ceasing to resist *what is* and giving up the need for control.

When you fully accept all other people, places and things, without trying to change them to suit your needs, you can channel your energy into what's really important; the things you *can* change. The only thing you're completely in control of is yourself. Since you cannot change others, only yourself, it makes sense that the most important relationship you have is with yourself. Concentrate on becoming a better, happier person. You can advise people on what worked for you. Or better yet, show them by example. But in the end they'll come to their own conclusions. See where you can make a difference, but don't waste your efforts trying to force what you can't. It'll only hurt you in the end.

Self-Compassion

One of the most important lessons I've learned is this: never overreact or beat yourself up about things. It only makes matters worse for everyone involved. Choose to be self-compassionate instead. Self-compassion means to accept responsibility for yourself, your actions and your experiences, without allowing yourself to feel bad about them.

Dr. R. Leary, a professor of psychology and neuroscience at Duke University, explains that self-compassion "helps to eliminate a lot of the anger, depression and pain we experience when things go badly for us" **According to Dr. Leary, there are three components to self-compassion:**

- Self-kindness (vs. being self-critical)
- Common humanity (viewing one's negative experiences as a normal)
- Mindful acceptance (vs. over-identifying with painful thoughts, feelings and experiences)

He goes on to explain that self-compassion "seems to be more important than self-esteem, and is in fact responsible for many of the positive benefits typically attributed to high self-esteem." Self-compassion is an essential part of self-esteem. When you're more self-compassionate you will have more confidence and will be more likely to set and accomplish your goals.

<hr>

What's done is done. What is just is.

<hr>

One day while in my kitchen I hit my head on a cupboard door that was left open. Immediately I became angry at the door, as if it was the door's fault for being open. Then something dawned on me; something so simple and yet so fundamental to my self-esteem. It wasn't the door's fault that I hit my head; it was *mine* for leaving it open.

A light went on that day, and from then on I have always made an effort to live my life with self-compassion. Don't get me wrong, I'm no Mother Teresa. But self-compassion has taught me to be kinder, softer, and more forgiving with myself and others; especially those closest to me. Self-compassion has blessed me with a new calmness and self-awareness I never knew I was capable of, but always craved. Being more self-compassionate has also helped me understand that I am not a victim of life's circumstances. I am in control of my reactions to them, and therefore have the ability to influence the outcome.

Spilt milk is usually nothing more than spilt milk. Accident or no accident, it's no big deal. Move on to more important things (your goals, your family, yourself, the moment . . .). Stop resisting what you cannot change and start living to affect what you can!

Accountability

Accountability is about taking responsibility for your life and the changes that need to be made. Being accountable means you stop looking to others to change your life; it means doing it yourself.

This morning my eldest son took away his little brother's toy. When he was told to give it back, he started to cry. This developed into a heated discussion between my husband, my son and me that lasted until we dropped him off at school. The problem is this; at times my son can be somewhat "spoiled". It's easy to blame him for his behavior, but the question remains; how did he become spoiled in the first place? Someone must have put it into his head that he was entitled to the toy and everything else he demands.

I could have told my husband that our son was born that way, or that he must have learned this behavior from his friends. But I would have been lying. Passing the buck would only delay or worsen our problem. Finding a solution was my only goal, so I did what needed to be done. I became accountable. I stepped up to the plate and admitted I was responsible.

See, when my second child was born, I felt a tremendous sense of guilt about not spending as much time with my first. Instead of disappointing him further, I created a habit of giving him whatever he wanted, whenever he wanted it. This behavioral issue was in fact my doing, not his. Avoidance does not solve problems; solutions solve problems. So, as painful as it was going to be, I was going to have to do the work necessary to fix the mess I created.

⚜

God, Grant me the serenity to accept the things I cannot change,
Courage to change the things I can,
And wisdom to know the difference.

—REINHOLD NIEBUHR—

⚜

When something bad happens, instead of feeling bad about it, learn from your choices and become accountable. Resolve to try your best to do things differently the next time. For example, if you don't feel good after yelling at your kids, it was probably the wrong way to deal with things. Accept responsibility for your part in it. Thank God for the experience, understanding that somehow you can positively benefit from it. Give yourself a dose of self-compassion and vow to try a different course of action next time. Thank God for giving you an opportunity to realize your faults and for His guidance. Ask Him to help you learn from your mistakes so you may become better next time. Then move forward with your newfound wisdom.

We all have an inner voice. It tells us, unfailingly, when we're thinking or acting in a positive, productive manner, and also when we're not. When something doesn't *feel* right, that means it probably isn't very good for you. This is your intuition talking to you. If you don't know this voice, continue to practice gratitude and soon it will come. Listen to it. Be accountable to it. It will never steer you wrong.

Action

Since we've spoken about action already, there really is no need to go into great detail about it here. But *action* is obviously a very important step, and maybe the most important of all. Without it nothing gets done. Solution oriented people tend to see a problem as an opportunity to take action. They waste little time and energy figuring out who is to blame. Instead they concentrate on the solution—what it is *they* can do to make things better.

Action is the step by which we take the first three A's and turn them into proactive behavior and palpable results.

I'm writing this book because I want to share with you my insight and experience, in the hope that it will inspire you to take meaningful action in your own life. I want you to know that I didn't just wake up one morning and find that my life was perfect. It all started when I acknowledged that there was a problem. I became accountable by admitting that the problem lay with me and my perceptions. I took action by *using* the amazing power of gratitude.

The book you hold in your hands is living proof that the principles I've laid out here do in fact work. I used to be a tired, bitter, bankrupt housewife. And now I am creating the life of my dreams. Thanks to gratitude, God, and goal setting, I am now able to recognize and then overcome blocks which keep me from my destiny. My intuition has now increased to the point where I can take responsibility for my faults before they wreak havoc. I've come to recognize minor upsets as just that; *minor*. I know that with every temporary defeat, an opportunity for growth awaits. I now have amazing peace of mind and a quiet self-assurance that fills me in every way. No longer do I worry about the future, instead I confidently take action to produce results. And my relationship with my family, myself, and God is stronger than I ever thought imaginable.

Is my life perfect? No. Am I happy? Yes. I am happy because one day at a time I actively work towards the perfection I seek. And in return, I gain and grow, gain and grow. I am still amazed how one small success—that single moment when I said my first "thank you" to my Higher Power—spread; infecting my entire being with love, passion, hope, faith, and a burning determination to become the change I dream of.

You have no need to feel jealous, less deserving or capable, or owed in this lifetime. You may not have the same advantages as another, but you definitely have the same opportunities. Create the life you were meant to live today by . . .

Applying the Four A's to Your Life

Let's say it's a sunny day and you're at the park with your dog. He seems to be having a wonderful time frolicking with all the other dogs. But something's wrong. You're feeling irritable. No matter how hard you try, you can't stop thinking about all the work waiting for you at home. Although playing with Sparky should be a good thing, you can't seem to ignore that nagging voice telling you that you should be somewhere else.

Let's break down this situation using the Four A's of Personal Development:

1. Awareness: In the middle of the stress, stop and admit that something's wrong. You can feel it. Don't ignore or deny it.

2. Acceptance: Stop fighting and resisting the dog and the fact you're not at home working. Breathe. Allow yourself to be in the moment—at the park, in the sunshine, with your dog who is simply ecstatic to be outdoors. Be grateful for the opportunity to spend time with him and for all the fun he's having (and that you could be having too). Know that your work will still be waiting for you when you get home.

3. Accountability: Step back for a moment and take full responsibility for how you are feeling. Whether it was your idea or not, you walked him there; not the other way around; so take account-ability for your irritability. Don't blame it on Sparky. No matter what's going on in your head, you're where *you chose* to be.

4. Action: Do something to change the way you feel. Create a goal to help you get what you want. For example, determine an exact time when you're going home. Be firm on that time. Until then, *be* in the moment, knowing that your needs will be taken care of soon. In the meanwhile, choose to be grate-ful for this precious time. Play with man's best friend *on his terms;* toss the ball or go for a walk. Smile. Laugh. Enjoy. Leave the park exactly when you said you would and when you get home, get straight to work.

A life of peace, happiness and success can only be achieved through balance of the body, mind and spirit. How good can you feel if you have poor health? How fulfilled are you really if you spend all day and night working? How successful can you be if your family is crammed into a one room apartment? How can you be at peace if your marriage is on shaky ground? How happy can you be if your children feel neglected? How strong can your faith be if you believe God is jealous, spiteful and punishing?

Your mind, body and spirit are interconnected. In order to achieve overall happiness and well-being, you must maintain a balance. Know that there is a time for work and a time for rest and play. Set, and aspire to meet your personal and professional goals every day, but be mindful of your need to spend time with your family and friends, going for walks in the sunshine with your dog, resting, getting massages, paying bills, or simply reading a good book (or even a trashy Hollywood magazine!).

Be Willing to Change

In the end, perhaps the biggest change we can make is to become *willing to change.*

Willingness is crucial when you're looking to grow. You can't change if you're not willing to let go of your old ways, if you're not willing to accept there is another way, and if you're not willing to give it a try.

Have you ever reached for a piece of chocolate cake and said, "I have no willpower. I have to have it?" People often say that they lack willpower. The truth is that we exert our willpower all the time. Sometimes we just choose to exert it on the wrong things—things which go against what we say we want. Exerting your willpower the right way involves coming out of your comfort zone. It may be painful at first, doing something you're not used to, but once you take that first step, and it really is only that—one quick exertion—a new habit will be on its way to being formed.

Once you make that decision and act on it, whether it be for one minute or one hour, that uncomfortable feeling will lessen and the likelihood of you sticking with it will increase. But the most important step is the first one—you just need to start! The solution is to exert your willpower by making that start every single day. If you find yourself quitting, try again tomorrow, and then the next day, and the next. Eventually, if it's worthwhile, for as long as you keep trying, that new habit will stick.

Each new day is another chance for you to choose. Are you going to choose the new way or the old way? One of the reasons the *Gratitude and Goals* Daily Journal so effectively ensures you achieve your goals is that it provides you with an opportunity to start again, every single day. The moment you begin writing, it compels you to move past your comfort zone so that you make the right decision; every day. Day-after-day, as you stick with it, the time you use to write in your journal will become a natural part of your day (and so will all the miraculous benefits that come from it).

Make a conscious *effort* throughout your day to become the change you seek. In other words, be *willing* to change. Remind yourself of your goals and structure your day so that you can achieve them. Changing the way you think and feel takes time and practice. Always aim to be the best you can be, but expect that you'll screw up from time to time. And when you fall down, get right back up and try again.

True happiness starts on the inside; all the material stuff is just the icing on the cake. It doesn't matter how much money, friends or lovers you have, or whether you were educated at an Ivy League school. If you're not truly at peace with who you are on the inside, no amount of "stuff" can ever make you feel whole. Only a life devoted to personal growth and joy can do that.

I came across a paragraph in the "Big Book" of Alcoholics Anonymous that perfectly summed up life and the pursuit of personal growth. I changed it somewhat to suit my needs. It went something like this:

We all want to be good. No one wants to be angry, fearful, resentful or untrusting. Negative feelings such as these block our connection with the good in the world. Most of us would change if we knew how, and if we knew it would be easy. You need only have an open, positive mind and the willingness to try without ever giving up. Be the best you that you can possibly be every day. That's all anyone can expect of you, including yourself.

CHAPTER FIFTEEN

TODAY I WOULD LIKE TO CHANGE THE FOLLOWING THINGS ABOUT MYSELF

"The whole point of being alive is to evolve into the complete person you were intended to be."

—OPRAH WINFREY—

Money does buy happiness. But it only buys continued happiness for those who were content before they had any! In order to savor the rewards that come with achieving your goals, it's best to first clear up some things that may keep you from truly enjoying them. These are the things that, if improved upon, would enhance your overall outlook, happiness and inner peace.

This is the part of your *Gratitude and Goals* Daily Journal where the Four A's of Personal Development get put into daily practice. Here, a passionate life filled with inner peace, love and enduring bliss is no longer just a possibility; it becomes reality.

The words you write in this section will serve as a conscious reminder of the negative thoughts and other obstacles that are blocking your success. With each new day, as you strive for personal development, you will begin to see a noticeable increase in your awareness and intuition, recognize and then eliminate internal roadblocks and ward off struggles from your life, even before they happen. You will build a kinder, more confident and intimate relationship with yourself and your Higher Power. And with every honest attempt at change, a more accepting, calm, loving and confident person will be revealed.

Becoming the Change

Change does not mean becoming someone you're not. It does not mean giving up those unique qualities which make you who you are either. To improve upon, or change who you are, is an on-going process which involves digging away the many layers of unwanted "debris"—the overbearing negativities and shortcomings—which overshadows your spectacular attributes.

We all have the ability to love, but some hearts are tainted by betrayal. We all have the talent to succeed, but some egos are bruised by fear or failure. We all have the capacity to be happy, but some souls are burdened with anger and resentment. Not only are we capable of having these wonderful things; we are meant to have them.

If you are ready to change, you must become accountable to the process of making the change. Start by becoming consciously aware of the things you would like to improve upon, or change (and in some cases, completely remove) about yourself. Then accept that whatever "it" is, it's not working for you, but against you. If you're not sure what changes should be made, pay close attention to your *true* feelings. They are a reflection of your deep desires and the window to your soul. When in doubt, stop and listen to the truth behind them; what is really going on inside you, not what your mind is telling you to feel.

It's not enough to simply say, "I'm just in a bad mood today." Dig deeper. Why are you in a bad mood? Is your anger really justified? Is there a part of you which knows you're just being self-centered? What do you really want? Are you really as strong as you'd like others to believe you are, or is your tough exterior nothing but a mask to protect your fragile core? Is it worth feeling this way or would it make better sense to deal with—better yet, *change* whatever is causing you to feel this way?

Working through each step of your *Gratitude and Goals* Daily Journal will solidify your responsibility, and act as a reminder of your commitment to a better you.

How Your *Gratitude and Goals* Daily Journal Encourages Change

Every day, when you write in this section of your *Gratitude and Goals* Daily Journal, you will be compelled to ask yourself, "What improvements or changes to my thoughts, feelings or behavior would I need to make today, in order to receive positive changes in my inner and outer worlds?"

With pen in hand, think about the kind of person you want to be. Keep it simple. There's no need to get too analytical, or tackle too much, too soon. Instead of dwelling on the negatives, gratefully acknowledge each one as a new opportunity for new growth.

There are many ways you can change yourself today. Here are just a few suggestions:

Do you want to be more grateful?

Do you want to have more faith?

Do you want to laugh more and be less angry?

Do you want to give more freely with fewer expectations?

Do you want to have more confidence to believe you are capable of anything?

Do you want to be more loving and kind?

Do you want to be more loyal, reliable or trustworthy?

Do you want to forgive more and resent less?

Do you want to be less judgmental, critical or envious of others?

Do you want to be more proactive; to work more effectively, not harder?

Do you want to be completely honest with yourself and others?

Do you want to be more patient?

Do you want to relax more?

Do you want to accept more and expect less?

Do you want to be more optimistic?

Do you want to be more creative?

Do you want to be on time, all the time?

Do you want to be a better listener?

Do you want to take responsibility for your actions?

Do you want to make amends to someone for something you did?

Do you want to be more courageous and less fearful?

Do you want to live your purpose more fully?

Do you want to start living in the moment; to be happy with whatever is happening now?

Becoming the person you want to be is an ongoing process, not an event. Start slowly. Commit to working on improving no more than one or two things each day. Some days you'll strive simply to smile or laugh more and that will be enough. There will also be days when you wish you could have a complete personality overhaul. But if you try to take on too much too soon, you'll have difficulties focusing and nothing will change. So again . . . keep it simple!

Here are some of the improvements I've written in my own *Gratitude and Goals* Daily Journal:

Today I would like to change, the following things about myself . . .

Be grateful for more; more often.

Smile more. Laugh more. Be lighter. Have more fun.

Admit it when I'm wrong. Apologize when it's my fault.

Live in the moment. Accept and appreciate everything and everyone in it.

Treat everyone as though they are important.

Spend my time wisely, not wastefully.

As with all the other sections of your *Gratitude and Goals* Daily Journal, this one requires action! When such negativities arise become aware of them, and then, without hesitation, do what's needed in that moment to create a change. Whatever the issue, the solution may be as simple as reversing your current pattern of thinking or behaving. Most times we simply need to notice our habits and deliberately reverse them. Just by offering a compliment, smile or apology when we would normally remain silent, for example, we can put an incredible charge in our inner life and our outer world. If you're impatient, work at being more patient. If you're an angry person, remind yourself that not everything is a big deal. In the end, your anger is only causing more pain. Commit to being more understanding and accepting.

If you find you're struggling, try turning it over to God. Ask that He remove the difficulty from your life. Every time it comes up, ask over and over again until it is gone. You may not be "healed" the first few times you try, but remember, God gives you opportunities. Instead of feeling bad, use this moment as a springboard for real growth. This is your chance to do the right thing.

⌐≈⋘⋙≈¬

"I don't think much of a man who is not wiser today
than he was yesterday."

—ABRAHAM LINCOLN—

⌐≈⋘⋙≈¬

Allow your desire for growth to guide your thoughts and behavior throughout the day. Practice *being* the person you want to be *in all your interactions*. Each day that you do so will bring you one step closer to enlightenment, to yourself, and to God. Soon you will no longer just be practicing. This new way of being will *become* your way of life.

Make a conscious effort to switch your thoughts towards the positive pole of whatever negativity you encounter. Of course, if you're going through a major tragedy, take the time you need to deal with it. Emotion *felt*, no matter what that emotion is, is good for the soul. In other words, don't suppress emotions; feel them. Allow them to *be*, but do not *become* them. Experience your emotions but know there must come a point when you need to move on.

We've talked a lot about plans and goals throughout this book. Still, all of our planning and goal setting must be weighed against one very important consideration. We can only see what we're capable of seeing at this stage of our development. The fascinating thing about personal development is that as *we* change, our needs and goals often change, too, in unpredictable ways. And as we adjust our needs, our course of personal growth may require minor or major adjustments from time to time as well.

Seemingly earth shattering revelations can be quickly forgotten if we don't record them. Write them down in a journal if it helps, but know that the critical thing about insights is to *use* them. If you start to get a strong gut sense that you are off-kilter, pay close attention to that feeling. Let it guide you in readjusting your ways.

Life is a journey. Listen to your feelings; know your truth. And live each day as though you are on the greatest adventure. It's your life, what could possibly be greater?

Create Habits that Last a Lifetime

If there's something you really want to change about yourself, make a point of writing it in your *Gratitude and Goals* Daily Journal, every day, for twenty-one consecutive days. Old patterns require conscious effort to break. It might take you simply replacing the old one with something new or it may take a hundred tries before a new behavior replaces the old. But with steady effort and self-compassion, the gift of a new freedom will be yours. Once you feel you've incorporated the change (to the best of your ability) into your life, move on to something new. With each victory, your reasons to be grateful will increase. And in return, so will your feelings of gratitude.

Today I choose to live my life in accordance with personal growth. I'm constantly looking for my accountability in matters *good and bad,* and looking for ways in which I can improve myself. But there are many times when I catch myself acting or thinking in a way that makes me uncomfortable. I feel myself slipping into old patterns and I don't like it. Those are the times I stop and check myself. *Was I being judgmental? Was I putting unrealistic expectations on myself or another? Did I pass blame instead of accepting responsibility? Did I make a big deal out of nothing? Did I miss a beautiful moment by wishing I was somewhere else?*

We're all works in progress. All we can do is the best we can. See your imperfections as stumbling blocks that ultimately stand in the way of your own happiness. Have the courage to let them go. If that seems impossible, pray to have them removed. Allow your desire for growth to guide your thoughts and behavior. With no further purpose in your life, damaging thoughts which once consumed you will soon be replaced by a newfound confidence, hope and enthusiasm.

You will gain a new, affirmative way of thinking. Your heart will open and your relationships will flourish. Your stress levels will go down and you will feel much lighter and more at peace than ever. Passion and success will come to you . . . *in all areas of your life.*

CHAPTER SIXTEEN

TO-DO'S

"Do not let what you cannot do interfere
with what you can do."

—JOHN WOODEN—

At the beginning of this book, I made a promise to you that I intend to keep. I said *if* you work through the *Gratitude and Goals* Daily Journal every day, you will become a "completer" in all areas of your life. Well, it wouldn't be much of a promise unless there was a section in your journal dedicated to tying up loose ends. Here's where we keep that promise: the *To-do's* section of your *Gratitude and Goals* Daily Journal.

Why do some people seem to have all the time in the world while others always complain they have none? No matter who they are, where they live, or what they do, every person in this world has one thing in common—*time!* We all have exactly twenty-four hours in a day to do the things that need to be done. Oprah, Bill Gates and Donald Trump all have twenty-four hours in a day. Gandhi, Mother Teresa and Martin Luther King, Jr. all did too. Remember that and you'll never allow yourself to use the excuse, "I don't have enough time" again. It's not how much time you have that counts, it's what you *do* with it that makes a difference.

"Lack of time is actually a lack of priorities."

—TIM FERRISS—

Throughout this book, I've stressed the importance of taking time out for you, so that your dreams and goals become a priority. But being goal-oriented doesn't give you a pass to ignore all the other daily tasks and to-do's that require your attention. These duties are just as important as your daily goals, and in some cases more so. If they weren't, the groceries would never be purchased, your pay checks would never get deposited, the weekly phone call to your mother might be forgotten, and you might put off paying your rent.

How can something like putting off going to the doctor or not paying your bills on time weigh you down and potentially sidetrack your goals? Do you remember the Universal Law of Non-Resistance? "What you resist, persists!" That tingling feeling in your arm isn't going away just because you choose to ignore it. And bill collectors won't stop calling your house just because you decided you can't pay them *right now*. I know from experience—they won't!

You can't deny reality and you can't avoid the inevitable. The longer you put something off, the more you will inevitably stress about it. What a waste of time! Being forgetful is not an excuse. Being too busy is not getting the job done either. Giving those things focus-time will! If you were to take a few minutes every day to write down all those things which need attending to, you can spend the rest of your day actually *getting them done.*

Think of a written to-do list as an extension of your goals—a very useful time management tool used to ensure success in all areas of your life. It's not about dwelling on those things which tend to weigh on you day in and day out. It's about getting them done so that you can live without any unnecessary stress. A concise to-do list will not only act as a written reminder of those things which require your attention, but also as an aid in managing your entire day. And when each task is complete you will feel the high of accomplishment, just as you do when you achieve your goals.

It's important to prioritize your to-do list by making sure that only the things that *should* be done that day are on it. Otherwise you may wind up with too many things to do, and none of them getting done.

You know something should be a priority if:
- It is imperative it gets done today.
- It will improve the quality of your life.
- It will weigh on your mind if it doesn't get done.
- It will aid in your personal growth.

Here's an example of some of the things that might make it to your list:

Pick up the dry cleaning

Meet Alex at the coffee shop at 2 p.m.

Sign up Julie for soccer

Pay the phone bill

Call Phil back about the meeting next week

Make an appointment for the cat's check-up

Meditate for ten minutes at lunch

If something's a top priority, tackle it just like you do your daily goals. And if for some reason it doesn't get done, be sure to put it on the next day's list. You can't sweep these things under the carpet. They exist, and if you try to minimize or ignore them they'll continue to build up over time and encourage feelings of inadequacy and failure. And the simple fact is, if you skimp here, you will probably be lackadaisical about your goals too.

If you let important tasks go unattended for too long, pressures can build up and you leave yourself open to a potential slip in personal growth. Embarrassment, guilt, or the need to blame may creep in, and that haunted feeling of an incomplete task will remain (until it's dealt with). That's not personal growth; that's personal regression.

Chapter Seventeen

NOTES AND INSPIRATIONS

"A word is a bud attempting to become a twig.
How can one not dream while writing?
It is the pen which dreams.
The blank page gives the right to dream."

—GASTON BACHELARD—

Wow, it's been such an incredible journey up to now, wouldn't you agree? First, we revealed the path to heightened spirituality, happiness and confidence, via the ongoing practice of gratitude. Then we discussed how to achieve anything you set your mind to by setting and actively pursuing goals. We topped it off with a hefty dose of self-awareness and personal development. And finally, we discovered the secret to being a "completer," so that you can be successful in all areas of your life. But wait, we're not quite finished yet! There's just one more section to look at before we're done . . .

Earlier I explained that true happiness cannot exist without balance—spiritually, emotionally, intellectually and physically. Balance includes all aspects of your life and cannot exist if there are parts left unaccounted for. The *Notes and Inspirations* section of your journal concludes our mission to achieve such balance by focusing on the more *creative* thoughts and feelings which linger inside you, pleading to come out.

This area is your section to do with whatever your heart desires. Use it to advance your life in some way, or at least make it easier.

As the title suggests, use this area as:

- A place to record daily affirmations
- A memo pad to jot down important numbers, favorite quotes, book titles, dates, memos to dictate, etc.
- A place to record ideas or inspirations you may have throughout your day. e.g., companies to contact, equations, recipes, etc.
- A progress log to keep track of specific developments and accomplishments, e.g., how much writing you did, your workout at the gym (how many reps/sets you did and of what), your meals if you are monitoring what you eat, prayers, writing, reading, homework, smoke-free days, weight lost, money earned, goals achieved, how many dates you had, etc.
- A calendar to keep track of the days you've been working through this program or any other new habit you're attempting to instill.
- Doodling, sketching, vision boarding, etc.

Whether you choose to use this section as a memo pad, a calendar, a progress log or as your private therapist, it doesn't really matter what you choose to write here. This is *your* space to do with want you want. And hey, you can even leave it blank. Some days I do.

A QUICK SUMMARY

Your *Gratitude And Goals* Daily Journal

"Everyone who got where he is
has had to begin where he was."

—ROBERT LOUIS STEVENSON—

From gratitude and goals to personal growth and tasks, it's all together on one page for you: the *Gratitude and Goals* Daily Journal page. Here is a quick section by section summary of how to best work through your *Gratitude and Goals* Daily Journal, so that you can get the most out of it and achieve all you've ever dreamed of.

Today's Date . . .

Even the date can be significant when it comes to achieving the life of your dreams.

For example, whenever I am going after a goal of twenty-one days, trying to create a habit out of a new behavior, I mark each day by writing its number (day #1, 2, 3 . . . 21) in the upper right hand corner of the page. This way I can be honest about my progress; making sure to start all over at day one if I missed a day.

Use the date as a meaningful way to keep yourself on track and accountable.

Today's date can also be used as a calendar for scheduling goals, tasks or events.

Today I am grateful for . . .

The purpose of this section is to shift your thinking toward the positive, open you up to new possibilities, and move you to a closer relationship with God.

There are literally millions of reasons why you can be grateful. Here you only need to pick four.

Briefly state what or whom you're grateful for. Say "Thank you" for that person, thing or situation. Consciously acknowledge that you're grateful to someone or something (a Divine Source) greater than you. Most importantly, give focus to specifically *why* you're grateful (i.e., the benefits to you). That's where the real feelings of gratitude kick in.

- Be sure to be grateful for all areas of your life, paying special attention to those things that reflect upon your goals.

- Be grateful for the past, present and future.

- Be grateful with meaning. Don't just write the words; *feel* grateful.

- Always be grateful in advance for at least one thing you anticipate will come to you in the future.

- Nothing puts you in the "love frequency" like expressing gratitude with heartfelt honesty.

My short term goals are . . .

A short term goal is a destination. Each one provides you a sense of direction and purpose. One-by-one, with each success, your short term goals will eventually lead you to fulfilling your long term goals, and ultimately your vision of the future.

Write achievements you want to realize within the next few days, weeks or months.

- Be brief but specific. Dates, timelines and other plans can change, but for the moment, it's important you know exactly *what* you want.

- Your short term goals are the foundation for your daily goals.

My daily goals are . . .

Daily goals are the best way to keep moving in the direction you want to be going. Day-by-day, with each success, you gain confidence, courage, experience and momentum towards achieving your short term goals.

Write your daily goals with purpose and an unswerving commitment to their achievement.

- Unless there's something else that requires your immediate attention, at least one of your daily goals should build toward one of your short term goals.

- Again, be specific. The more focused you are, the greater your chance of success.

Action steps . . .

Each action step is a small but important accomplishment, building toward the completion of your daily goal.

Write at least one action step for each of your daily goals. Be as specific as possible (e.g., "Write from 1 p.m. to 3 p.m." or "Run three miles").

Always keep in mind when writing your goals:

- Make a point to record your progress if it helps you to stay committed.

- Attempt to make up any lost time or shortfalls so that you complete your daily goals.
- Do your best always, but don't beat yourself up if sometimes you miss the mark.

Today I would like to change the following things about myself . . .

No one likes *everything* about themselves. I'm sure even David Beckham looks himself in the mirror some days and sees things he wishes he could change! Consider this section to be your personal therapy office; the place where you're totally honest about what's really going on in your head. Take the first step to becoming the person you want to be by admitting your less than perfect thoughts, emotions and actions. Acknowledging them will put *you* in control of changing them.

Write down one, two or even a few (but not too many) positive changes you'll work toward that day.

- Be totally honest about your imperfections.
- Be responsible for your thoughts, feelings and actions; never blaming others for the way you think, feel or behave.
- Be the change you seek by reversing old patterns and creating new ones (e.g. Remember to be grateful. Live in the moment. Be more patient with my kids. Breathe!).
- Pray to God to help you be courageous enough to get through the struggles and setbacks.

To-do's . . .

This section is like a post-it note; a reminder to complete all the errands and non-goal-oriented tasks that need to be completed that day. To-do's can be just as important as your goals. Without their completion, life would be filled with loose ends that leave you feeling overwhelmed.

Write down anything, from your grocery list to important phone calls you want to make that day.

- Refer to this section as needed and check things off once completed, if this helps.
- If there's anything that wasn't done today, add it to your next day's list.
- Use this section to maintain a balance between goal achievement and life management.

Notes and Inspirations . . .

This section can be used like a progress report or mini-journal to record not only your daily successes, but also the obstacles that sometimes creep in to challenge you. It can also be used to record any interesting and meaningful insights that come up during the day.

- Record your progress toward a particular goal.
- Note any problems, struggles and resolutions.
- Jot down insights.
- Keep track of anything you want!

Remember: you are creating the life of your dreams here. Stay committed, never give up and most of all . . . have fun!

BOOK TWO

It's Time To Take Action

Today's Date: _____

Today I am grateful for:

1. _____

_____

2. _____

_____

3. _____

_____

4. _____

_____

My short term goals are:

1. _____

2. _____

My daily goals are:

1. _____

Action steps: _____

2. _____

Action steps: _____

3. _____

Action steps: _____

Today I would like to change the following things about myself:

1. _____

2. _____

3. _____

To-do's:

1. _____   4. _____

2. _____   5. _____

3. _____   6. _____

Notes and Inspirations: _____

_____

_____

Today's Date: _____

Today I am grateful for:

1. _____

_____

2. _____

_____

3. _____

_____

4. _____

_____

My short term goals are:

1. _____

2. _____

My daily goals are:

1. _____

Action steps: _____

2. _____

Action steps: _____

3. _____

Action steps: _____

Today I would like to change the following things about myself:

1. _____

2. _____

3. _____

To-do's:

1. _____ 4. _____

2. _____ 5. _____

3. _____ 6. _____

Notes and Inspirations: _____

_____

_____

Today's Date: _____

Today I am grateful for:

1._____

_____

2._____

_____

3._____

_____

4._____

_____

My short term goals are:

1._____

2._____

My daily goals are:

1._____

Action steps: _____

2._____

Action steps: _____

3._____

Action steps: _____

Today I would like to change the following things about myself:

1._____

2._____

3._____

To-do's:

1._____   4._____

2._____   5._____

3._____   6._____

Notes and Inspirations:_____

_____

_____

Today's Date: _____

Today I am grateful for:

1._____

_____

2._____

_____

3._____

_____

4._____

_____

My short term goals are:

1._____

2._____

My daily goals are:

1._____

Action steps: _____

2._____

Action steps: _____

3._____

Action steps: _____

Today I would like to change the following things about myself:

1._____

2._____

3._____

To-do's:

1._____   4._____

2._____   5._____

3._____   6._____

Notes and Inspirations:_____

_____

_____

Today's Date: _____

Today I am grateful for:

1._____

_____

2._____

_____

3._____

_____

4._____

_____

My short term goals are:

1._____

2._____

My daily goals are:

1._____

Action steps: _____

2._____

Action steps: _____

3._____

Action steps: _____

Today I would like to change the following things about myself:

1._____

2._____

3._____

To-do's:

1._____   4._____

2._____   5._____

3._____   6._____

Notes and Inspirations:_____

_____

_____

Today's Date: _____

Today I am grateful for:

1._____

_____

2._____

_____

3._____

_____

4._____

_____

My short term goals are:

1._____

2._____

My daily goals are:

1._____

Action steps: _____

2._____

Action steps: _____

3._____

Action steps: _____

Today I would like to change the following things about myself:

1._____

2._____

3._____

To-do's:

1._____   4._____

2._____   5._____

3._____   6._____

Notes and Inspirations:_____

_____

_____

Today's Date: _____

Today I am grateful for:

1._____

_____

2._____

_____

3._____

_____

4._____

_____

My short term goals are:

1._____

2._____

My daily goals are:

1._____

Action steps: _____

2._____

Action steps: _____

3._____

Action steps: _____

Today I would like to change the following things about myself:

1._____

2._____

3._____

To-do's:

1._____   4._____

2._____   5._____

3._____   6._____

Notes and Inspirations:_____

_____

_____

Today's Date: _____

Today I am grateful for:

1._____

_____

2._____

_____

3._____

_____

4._____

_____

My short term goals are:

1._____

2._____

My daily goals are:

1._____

Action steps: _____

2._____

Action steps: _____

3._____

Action steps: _____

Today I would like to change the following things about myself:

1._____

2._____

3._____

To-do's:

1._____   4._____

2._____   5._____

3._____   6._____

Notes and Inspirations:_____

_____

_____

Today's Date: _____

Today I am grateful for:

1._____

_____

2._____

_____

3._____

_____

4._____

_____

My short term goals are:

1._____

2._____

My daily goals are:

1._____

Action steps: _____

2._____

Action steps: _____

3._____

Action steps: _____

Today I would like to change the following things about myself:

1._____

2._____

3._____

To-do's:

1._____   4._____

2._____   5._____

3._____   6._____

Notes and Inspirations:_____

_____

_____

Today's Date: _____

Today I am grateful for:

1._____

_____

2._____

_____

3._____

_____

4._____

_____

My short term goals are:

1._____

2._____

My daily goals are:

1._____

Action steps: _____

2._____

Action steps: _____

3._____

Action steps: _____

Today I would like to change the following things about myself:

1._____

2._____

3._____

To-do's:

1._____   4._____

2._____   5._____

3._____   6._____

Notes and Inspirations:_____

_____

_____

Today's Date: _____

Today I am grateful for:

1._____

_____

2._____

_____

3._____

_____

4._____

_____

My short term goals are:

1._____

2._____

My daily goals are:

1._____

Action steps: _____

2._____

Action steps: _____

3._____

Action steps: _____

Today I would like to change the following things about myself:

1._____

2._____

3._____

To-do's:

1._____ 4._____

2._____ 5._____

3._____ 6._____

Notes and Inspirations:_____

_____

_____

Today's Date: _____

Today I am grateful for:

1._____

_____

2._____

_____

3._____

_____

4._____

_____

My short term goals are:

1._____

2._____

My daily goals are:

1._____

Action steps: _____

2._____

Action steps: _____

3._____

Action steps: _____

Today I would like to change the following things about myself:

1._____

2._____

3._____

To-do's:

1._____   4._____

2._____   5._____

3._____   6._____

Notes and Inspirations:_____

_____

_____

Today's Date: _____

Today I am grateful for:

1. _____

_____

2. _____

_____

3. _____

_____

4. _____

_____

My short term goals are:

1. _____

2. _____

My daily goals are:

1. _____

Action steps: _____

2. _____

Action steps: _____

3. _____

Action steps: _____

Today I would like to change the following things about myself:

1. _____

2. _____

3. _____

To-do's:

1. _____   4. _____

2. _____   5. _____

3. _____   6. _____

Notes and Inspirations: _____

_____

_____

Today's Date: _____

Today I am grateful for:

1._____

_____

2._____

_____

3._____

_____

4._____

_____

My short term goals are:

1._____

2._____

My daily goals are:

1._____

Action steps: _____

2._____

Action steps: _____

3._____

Action steps: _____

Today I would like to change the following things about myself:

1._____

2._____

3._____

To-do's:

1._____   4._____

2._____   5._____

3._____   6._____

Notes and Inspirations:_____

_____

_____

Today's Date: _____

Today I am grateful for:

1._____

_____

2._____

_____

3._____

_____

4._____

_____

My short term goals are:

1._____

2._____

My daily goals are:

1._____

Action steps: _____

2._____

Action steps: _____

3._____

Action steps: _____

Today I would like to change the following things about myself:

1._____

2._____

3._____

To-do's:

1._____ 4._____

2._____ 5._____

3._____ 6._____

Notes and Inspirations:_____

_____

_____

Today's Date: _____

Today I am grateful for:

1. _____

_____

2. _____

_____

3. _____

_____

4. _____

_____

My short term goals are:

1. _____

2. _____

My daily goals are:

1. _____

Action steps: _____

2. _____

Action steps: _____

3. _____

Action steps: _____

Today I would like to change the following things about myself:

1. _____

2. _____

3. _____

To-do's:

1. _____ 4. _____

2. _____ 5. _____

3. _____ 6. _____

Notes and Inspirations: _____

_____

_____

Today's Date: _____

Today I am grateful for:

1._____

_____

2._____

_____

3._____

_____

4._____

_____

My short term goals are:

1._____

2._____

My daily goals are:

1._____

Action steps: _____

2._____

Action steps: _____

3._____

Action steps: _____

Today I would like to change the following things about myself:

1._____

2._____

3._____

To-do's:

1._____   4._____

2._____   5._____

3._____   6._____

Notes and Inspirations:_____

_____

_____

Today's Date: _____

Today I am grateful for:

1._____

_____

2._____

_____

3._____

_____

4._____

_____

My short term goals are:

1._____

2._____

My daily goals are:

1._____

Action steps: _____

2._____

Action steps: _____

3._____

Action steps: _____

Today I would like to change the following things about myself:

1._____

2._____

3._____

To-do's:

1._____   4._____

2._____   5._____

3._____   6._____

Notes and Inspirations:_____

_____

_____

Today's Date: _____

Today I am grateful for:

1._____

_____

2._____

_____

3._____

_____

4._____

_____

My short term goals are:

1._____

2._____

My daily goals are:

1._____

Action steps: _____

2._____

Action steps: _____

3._____

Action steps: _____

Today I would like to change the following things about myself:

1._____

2._____

3._____

To-do's:

1._____   4._____

2._____   5._____

3._____   6._____

Notes and Inspirations:_____

_____

_____

Today's Date: _____

Today I am grateful for:

1._____

_____

2._____

_____

3._____

_____

4._____

_____

My short term goals are:

1._____

2._____

My daily goals are:

1._____

Action steps: _____

2._____

Action steps: _____

3._____

Action steps: _____

Today I would like to change the following things about myself:

1._____

2._____

3._____

To-do's:

1._____   4._____

2._____   5._____

3._____   6._____

Notes and Inspirations:_____

_____

_____

Today's Date: _____

Today I am grateful for:

1._____

_____

2._____

_____

3._____

_____

4._____

_____

My short term goals are:

1._____

2._____

My daily goals are:

1._____

Action steps: _____

2._____

Action steps: _____

3._____

Action steps: _____

Today I would like to change the following things about myself:

1._____

2._____

3._____

To-do's:

1._____   4._____

2._____   5._____

3._____   6._____

Notes and Inspirations:_____

_____

_____

Today's Date: _____

Today I am grateful for:

1._____

_____

2._____

_____

3._____

_____

4._____

_____

My short term goals are:

1._____

2._____

My daily goals are:

1._____

Action steps: _____

2._____

Action steps: _____

3._____

Action steps: _____

Today I would like to change the following things about myself:

1._____

2._____

3._____

To-do's:

1._____   4._____

2._____   5._____

3._____   6._____

Notes and Inspirations:_____

_____

_____

Today's Date: _____

Today I am grateful for:

1._____

_____

2._____

_____

3._____

_____

4._____

_____

My short term goals are:

1._____

2._____

My daily goals are:

1._____

Action steps: _____

2._____

Action steps: _____

3._____

Action steps: _____

Today I would like to change the following things about myself:

1._____

2._____

3._____

To-do's:

1._____   4._____

2._____   5._____

3._____   6._____

Notes and Inspirations:_____

_____

_____

Today's Date: _____

Today I am grateful for:

1._____

_____

2._____

_____

3._____

_____

4._____

_____

My short term goals are:

1._____

2._____

My daily goals are:

1._____

Action steps: _____

2._____

Action steps: _____

3._____

Action steps: _____

Today I would like to change the following things about myself:

1._____

2._____

3._____

To-do's:

1._____   4._____

2._____   5._____

3._____   6._____

Notes and Inspirations:_____

_____

_____

Today's Date: _____

Today I am grateful for:

1._____

_____

2._____

_____

3._____

_____

4._____

_____

My short term goals are:

1._____

2._____

My daily goals are:

1._____

Action steps: _____

2._____

Action steps: _____

3._____

Action steps: _____

Today I would like to change the following things about myself:

1._____

2._____

3._____

To-do's:

1._____   4._____

2._____   5._____

3._____   6._____

Notes and Inspirations:_____

_____

_____

Today's Date: _____

Today I am grateful for:

1._____

_____

2._____

_____

3._____

_____

4._____

_____

My short term goals are:

1._____

2._____

My daily goals are:

1._____

Action steps: _____

2._____

Action steps: _____

3._____

Action steps: _____

Today I would like to change the following things about myself:

1._____

2._____

3._____

To-do's:

1._____   4._____

2._____   5._____

3._____   6._____

Notes and Inspirations:_____

_____

_____

Today's Date: _____

Today I am grateful for:

1._____

_____

2._____

_____

3._____

_____

4._____

_____

My short term goals are:

1._____

2._____

My daily goals are:

1._____

Action steps: _____

2._____

Action steps: _____

3._____

Action steps: _____

Today I would like to change the following things about myself:

1._____

2._____

3._____

To-do's:

1._____   4._____

2._____   5._____

3._____   6._____

Notes and Inspirations:_____

_____

_____

Today's Date: _____

Today I am grateful for:

1._____

_____

2._____

_____

3._____

_____

4._____

_____

My short term goals are:

1._____

2._____

My daily goals are:

1._____

Action steps: _____

2._____

Action steps: _____

3._____

Action steps: _____

Today I would like to change the following things about myself:

1._____

2._____

3._____

To-do's:

1._____   4._____

2._____   5._____

3._____   6._____

Notes and Inspirations:_____

_____

_____

Today's Date: _____

Today I am grateful for:

1._____

_____

2._____

_____

3._____

_____

4._____

_____

My short term goals are:

1._____

2._____

My daily goals are:

1._____

Action steps: _____

2._____

Action steps: _____

3._____

Action steps: _____

Today I would like to change the following things about myself:

1._____

2._____

3._____

To-do's:

1._____   4._____

2._____   5._____

3._____   6._____

Notes and Inspirations:_____

_____

_____

Today's Date: _____

Today I am grateful for:

1._____

_____

2._____

_____

3._____

_____

4._____

_____

My short term goals are:

1._____

2._____

My daily goals are:

1._____

Action steps: _____

2._____

Action steps: _____

3._____

Action steps: _____

Today I would like to change the following things about myself:

1._____

2._____

3._____

To-do's:

1._____   4._____

2._____   5._____

3._____   6._____

Notes and Inspirations:_____

_____

_____

Today's Date: _____

Today I am grateful for:

1._____

_____

2._____

_____

3._____

_____

4._____

_____

My short term goals are:

1._____

2._____

My daily goals are:

1._____

Action steps: _____

2._____

Action steps: _____

3._____

Action steps: _____

Today I would like to change the following things about myself:

1._____

2._____

3._____

To-do's:

1._____   4._____

2._____   5._____

3._____   6._____

Notes and Inspirations:_____

_____

_____

Today's Date: _____

Today I am grateful for:

1._____

_____

2._____

_____

3._____

_____

4._____

_____

My short term goals are:

1._____

2._____

My daily goals are:

1._____

Action steps: _____

2._____

Action steps: _____

3._____

Action steps: _____

Today I would like to change the following things about myself:

1._____

2._____

3._____

To-do's:

1._____   4._____

2._____   5._____

3._____   6._____

Notes and Inspirations:_____

_____

_____

Today's Date: _____

Today I am grateful for:

1._____

_____

2._____

_____

3._____

_____

4._____

_____

My short term goals are:

1._____

2._____

My daily goals are:

1._____

Action steps: _____

2._____

Action steps: _____

3._____

Action steps: _____

Today I would like to change the following things about myself:

1._____

2._____

3._____

To-do's:

1._____   4._____

2._____   5._____

3._____   6._____

Notes and Inspirations:_____

_____

_____

Today's Date: _____

Today I am grateful for:

1._____

_____

2._____

_____

3._____

_____

4._____

_____

My short term goals are:

1._____

2._____

My daily goals are:

1._____

Action steps: _____

2._____

Action steps: _____

3._____

Action steps: _____

Today I would like to change the following things about myself:

1._____

2._____

3._____

To-do's:

1._____   4._____

2._____   5._____

3._____   6._____

Notes and Inspirations:_____

_____

_____

Today's Date: _____

Today I am grateful for:

1._____

_____

2._____

_____

3._____

_____

4._____

_____

My short term goals are:

1._____

2._____

My daily goals are:

1._____

Action steps: _____

2._____

Action steps: _____

3._____

Action steps: _____

Today I would like to change the following things about myself:

1._____

2._____

3._____

To-do's:

1._____	4._____
2._____	5._____
3._____	6._____

Notes and Inspirations:_____

_____

_____

Today's Date: _____

Today I am grateful for:

1._____

_____

2._____

_____

3._____

_____

4._____

_____

My short term goals are:

1._____

2._____

My daily goals are:

1._____

Action steps: _____

2._____

Action steps: _____

3._____

Action steps: _____

Today I would like to change the following things about myself:

1._____

2._____

3._____

To-do's:

1._____   4. _____

2._____   5._____

3._____   6._____

Notes and Inspirations:_____

_____

_____

Today's Date: _____

Today I am grateful for:

1._____

_____

2._____

_____

3._____

_____

4._____

_____

My short term goals are:

1._____

2._____

My daily goals are:

1._____

Action steps: _____

2._____

Action steps: _____

3._____

Action steps: _____

Today I would like to change the following things about myself:

1._____

2._____

3._____

To-do's:

1._____   4._____

2._____   5._____

3._____   6._____

Notes and Inspirations:_____

_____

_____

Today's Date: _____

Today I am grateful for:

1._____

_____

2._____

_____

3._____

_____

4._____

_____

My short term goals are:

1._____

2._____

My daily goals are:

1._____

Action steps: _____

2._____

Action steps: _____

3._____

Action steps: _____

Today I would like to change the following things about myself:

1._____

2._____

3._____

To-do's:

1._____   4._____

2._____   5._____

3._____   6._____

Notes and Inspirations:_____

_____

_____

Today's Date: _____

Today I am grateful for:

1. _____

_____

2. _____

_____

3. _____

_____

4. _____

_____

My short term goals are:

1. _____

2. _____

My daily goals are:

1. _____

Action steps: _____

2. _____

Action steps: _____

3. _____

Action steps: _____

Today I would like to change the following things about myself:

1. _____

2. _____

3. _____

To-do's:

1. _____   4. _____

2. _____   5. _____

3. _____   6. _____

Notes and Inspirations: _____

_____

_____

Today's Date: _____

Today I am grateful for:

1._____

_____

2._____

_____

3._____

_____

4._____

_____

My short term goals are:

1._____

2._____

My daily goals are:

1._____

Action steps: _____

2._____

Action steps: _____

3._____

Action steps: _____

Today I would like to change the following things about myself:

1._____

2._____

3._____

To-do's:

1._____   4._____

2._____   5._____

3._____   6._____

Notes and Inspirations:_____

_____

_____

Today's Date: _____

Today I am grateful for:

1._____

_____

2._____

_____

3._____

_____

4._____

_____

My short term goals are:

1._____

2._____

My daily goals are:

1._____

Action steps: _____

2._____

Action steps: _____

3._____

Action steps: _____

Today I would like to change the following things about myself:

1._____

2._____

3._____

To-do's:

1._____   4._____

2._____   5._____

3._____   6._____

Notes and Inspirations:_____

_____

_____

Today's Date: _____

Today I am grateful for:

1. _____

_____

2. _____

_____

3. _____

_____

4. _____

_____

My short term goals are:

1. _____

2. _____

My daily goals are:

1. _____

Action steps: _____

2. _____

Action steps: _____

3. _____

Action steps: _____

Today I would like to change the following things about myself:

1. _____

2. _____

3. _____

To-do's:

1. _____   4. _____

2. _____   5. _____

3. _____   6. _____

Notes and Inspirations: _____

_____

_____

Today's Date: _____

Today I am grateful for:

1. _____

_____

2. _____

_____

3. _____

_____

4. _____

_____

My short term goals are:

1. _____

2. _____

My daily goals are:

1. _____

Action steps: _____

2. _____

Action steps: _____

3. _____

Action steps: _____

Today I would like to change the following things about myself:

1. _____

2. _____

3. _____

To-do's:

1. _____   4. _____

2. _____   5. _____

3. _____   6. _____

Notes and Inspirations: _____

_____

_____

Today's Date: _____

Today I am grateful for:

1._____

_____

2._____

_____

3._____

_____

4._____

_____

My short term goals are:

1._____

2._____

My daily goals are:

1._____

Action steps: _____

2._____

Action steps: _____

3._____

Action steps: _____

Today I would like to change the following things about myself:

1._____

2._____

3._____

To-do's:

1._____   4._____

2._____   5._____

3._____   6._____

Notes and Inspirations:_____

_____

_____

Today's Date: _____

Today I am grateful for:

1._____

_____

2._____

_____

3._____

_____

4._____

_____

My short term goals are:

1._____

2._____

My daily goals are:

1._____

Action steps: _____

2._____

Action steps: _____

3._____

Action steps: _____

Today I would like to change the following things about myself:

1._____

2._____

3._____

To-do's:

1._____   4._____

2._____   5._____

3._____   6._____

Notes and Inspirations:_____

_____

_____

Today's Date: _____

Today I am grateful for:

1._____

_____

2._____

_____

3._____

_____

4._____

_____

My short term goals are:

1._____

2._____

My daily goals are:

1._____

Action steps: _____

2._____

Action steps: _____

3._____

Action steps: _____

Today I would like to change the following things about myself:

1._____

2._____

3._____

To-do's:

1._____   4._____

2._____   5._____

3._____   6._____

Notes and Inspirations:_____

_____

_____

Today's Date: _____

Today I am grateful for:

1._____

_____

2._____

_____

3._____

_____

4._____

_____

My short term goals are:

1._____

2._____

My daily goals are:

1._____

Action steps: _____

2._____

Action steps: _____

3._____

Action steps: _____

Today I would like to change the following things about myself:

1._____

2._____

3._____

To-do's:

1._____   4. _____

2._____   5._____

3._____   6._____

Notes and Inspirations:_____

_____

_____

Today's Date: _____

Today I am grateful for:

1._____

_____

2._____

_____

3._____

_____

4._____

_____

My short term goals are:

1._____

2._____

My daily goals are:

1._____

Action steps: _____

2._____

Action steps: _____

3._____

Action steps: _____

Today I would like to change the following things about myself:

1._____

2._____

3._____

To-do's:

1._____   4._____

2._____   5._____

3._____   6._____

Notes and Inspirations:_____

_____

_____

Today's Date: _____

Today I am grateful for:

1._____

_____

2._____

_____

3._____

_____

4._____

_____

My short term goals are:

1._____

2._____

My daily goals are:

1._____

Action steps: _____

2._____

Action steps: _____

3._____

Action steps: _____

Today I would like to change the following things about myself:

1._____

2._____

3._____

To-do's:

1._____   4._____

2._____   5._____

3._____   6._____

Notes and Inspirations:_____

_____

_____

Today's Date: _____

Today I am grateful for:

1._____

_____

2._____

_____

3._____

_____

4._____

_____

My short term goals are:

1._____

2._____

My daily goals are:

1._____

Action steps: _____

2._____

Action steps: _____

3._____

Action steps: _____

Today I would like to change the following things about myself:

1._____

2._____

3._____

To-do's:

1._____   4._____

2._____   5._____

3._____   6._____

Notes and Inspirations:_____

_____

_____

Today's Date: _____

Today I am grateful for:

1. _____

_____

2. _____

_____

3. _____

_____

4. _____

_____

My short term goals are:

1. _____

2. _____

My daily goals are:

1. _____

Action steps: _____

2. _____

Action steps: _____

3. _____

Action steps: _____

Today I would like to change the following things about myself:

1. _____

2. _____

3. _____

To-do's:

1. _____   4. _____

2. _____   5. _____

3. _____   6. _____

Notes and Inspirations: _____

_____

_____

Today's Date: _____

Today I am grateful for:

1._____

_____

2._____

_____

3._____

_____

4._____

_____

My short term goals are:

1._____

2._____

My daily goals are:

1._____

Action steps: _____

2._____

Action steps: _____

3._____

Action steps: _____

Today I would like to change the following things about myself:

1._____

2._____

3._____

To-do's:

1._____   4._____

2._____   5._____

3._____   6._____

Notes and Inspirations:_____

_____

_____

Today's Date: _____

Today I am grateful for:

1._____

_____

2._____

_____

3._____

_____

4._____

_____

My short term goals are:

1._____

2._____

My daily goals are:

1._____

Action steps: _____

2._____

Action steps: _____

3._____

Action steps: _____

Today I would like to change the following things about myself:

1._____

2._____

3._____

To-do's:

1._____   4._____

2._____   5._____

3._____   6._____

Notes and Inspirations:_____

_____

_____

Today's Date: _____

Today I am grateful for:

1._____
_____

2._____
_____

3._____
_____

4._____
_____

My short term goals are:

1._____

2._____

My daily goals are:

1._____

Action steps: _____

2._____

Action steps: _____

3._____

Action steps: _____

Today I would like to change the following things about myself:

1._____

2._____

3._____

To-do's:

1._____   4._____

2._____   5._____

3._____   6._____

Notes and Inspirations:_____
_____
_____

Today's Date: _____

Today I am grateful for:

1._____

_____

2._____

_____

3._____

_____

4._____

_____

My short term goals are:

1._____

2._____

My daily goals are:

1._____

Action steps: _____

2._____

Action steps: _____

3._____

Action steps: _____

Today I would like to change the following things about myself:

1._____

2._____

3._____

To-do's:

1._____   4._____

2._____   5._____

3._____   6._____

Notes and Inspirations:_____

_____

_____

Today's Date: _____

Today I am grateful for:

1. _____

_____

2. _____

_____

3. _____

_____

4. _____

_____

My short term goals are:

1. _____

2. _____

My daily goals are:

1. _____

Action steps: _____

2. _____

Action steps: _____

3. _____

Action steps: _____

Today I would like to change the following things about myself:

1. _____

2. _____

3. _____

To-do's:

1. _____ 4. _____

2. _____ 5. _____

3. _____ 6. _____

Notes and Inspirations: _____

_____

_____

Today's Date: _____

Today I am grateful for:

1._____

_____

2._____

_____

3._____

_____

4._____

_____

My short term goals are:

1._____

2._____

My daily goals are:

1._____

Action steps: _____

2._____

Action steps: _____

3._____

Action steps: _____

Today I would like to change the following things about myself:

1._____

2._____

3._____

To-do's:

1._____   4._____

2._____   5._____

3._____   6._____

Notes and Inspirations:_____

_____

_____

Today's Date: _____

Today I am grateful for:

1._____

_____

2._____

_____

3._____

_____

4._____

_____

My short term goals are:

1._____

2._____

My daily goals are:

1._____

Action steps: _____

2._____

Action steps: _____

3._____

Action steps: _____

Today I would like to change the following things about myself:

1._____

2._____

3._____

To-do's:

1._____   4._____

2._____   5._____

3._____   6._____

Notes and Inspirations:_____

_____

_____

Today's Date: _____

Today I am grateful for:

1._____

_____

2._____

_____

3._____

_____

4._____

_____

My short term goals are:

1._____

2._____

My daily goals are:

1._____

Action steps: _____

2._____

Action steps: _____

3._____

Action steps: _____

Today I would like to change the following things about myself:

1._____

2._____

3._____

To-do's:

1._____	4._____
2._____	5._____
3._____	6._____

Notes and Inspirations:_____

_____

_____

Today's Date: _____

Today I am grateful for:

1._____

_____

2._____

_____

3._____

_____

4._____

_____

My short term goals are:

1._____

2._____

My daily goals are:

1._____

Action steps: _____

2._____

Action steps: _____

3._____

Action steps: _____

Today I would like to change the following things about myself:

1._____

2._____

3._____

To-do's:

1._____   4._____

2._____   5._____

3._____   6._____

Notes and Inspirations:_____

_____

_____

Today's Date: _____

Today I am grateful for:

1._____

_____

2._____

_____

3._____

_____

4._____

_____

My short term goals are:

1._____

2._____

My daily goals are:

1._____

Action steps: _____

2._____

Action steps: _____

3._____

Action steps: _____

Today I would like to change the following things about myself:

1._____

2._____

3._____

To-do's:

1._____   4._____

2._____   5._____

3._____   6._____

Notes and Inspirations:_____

_____

_____

REFERENCES

PREFACE

Schucman, H 2007, *A Course in Miracles,* Combined Volume, Third Edition, Foundation for Inner Peace, Mill Valley, CA.

Heriot, D (Director) 2006, *The Secret,* Extended Edition, TS Productions LLC, Tuggeranong, Australia.

CHAPTER ONE

Casey, E & Mann, JD 2008, *'Why You Should Start a Business Today and Recession Proof Your Income',* Success Magazine, June/July, 55.

Maltz, Dr. M 2002, *The New Psycho-Cybernetics,* Prentice Hall Press, New York.

Peale, NV 1963, *The Power of Positive Thinking,* Fawcett Crest Books, New York.

Williamson, M 1993, *A Return to Love,* Harper Perennial, New York.

CHAPTER TWO

Shadyac, T (Director) 2007, *Evan Almighty,* Universal Studios, Universal City, CA.

Walsh, ND 1996, *Conversations with God,* Penguin Putnam Inc., New York.

CHAPTER THREE

Justice, Drs. B & R 2007, *'Giving Thanks: The Effects of Joy and Gratitude on the Human Body',* Successful Living Magazine, Autumn, 18-19.

CHAPTER FIVE

Dingle, Dr. P 2008, *Gratitude and Generosity,* www.kindredmedia.com.au.

CHAPTER SIX

Justice, Drs. B & J 2007, *'Giving Thanks: The Effects of Joy and Gratitude on the Human Body',* Successful Living Magazine, Autumn, 18-19.

CHAPTER NINE

Casey, E & Mann, JD 2008, *'Why You Should Start a Business Today and Recession Proof Your Income',* Success Magazine, June/July, 61.

Covey, SR 2004, *The 7 Habits of Highly Effective People,* Free Press, New York.

Hill, N 2005, *Think and Grow Rich,* Jeremy P. Tarcher/ Penguin, New York.

King, Jr., ML 1992, *I Have a Dream: Writings and Speeches That Changed the World,* Harper San Francisco, New York.

CHAPTER TEN

Ferriss, T 2007, *The 4-Hour Workweek,* Crown Publishers,
New York.

CHAPTER TWELVE

Munshi, PP 2009, *Set in Your Own Ways?,*
The Hindu Business Line, www.blonnet.com.

CHAPTER THIRTEEN

Maltz, M 1969, *Psycho-Cybernetics,* Pocket Books,
New York.

CHAPTER FOURTEEN

Alcoholics Anonymous 1976, 3rd Edition,
Alcoholics Anonymous World Services Inc., New York.

Leary, MR, Tate, EB, Adams, CE, Allen, AB, & Hancock,
J 2007, *'Self-Compassion and Reactions to Unpleasant Self-
relevant Events: The Implications of Treating Oneself Kindly',*
Journal of Personality and Social Psychology, May, 92,
887-904.

ABOUT THE AUTHOR

In her compelling debut book, *Gratitude and Goals*, Stacey Grewal skillfully teaches the art of triumphing over tragedy. Shortly after her family experienced a painful bankruptcy, she vowed never to fall victim to circumstance again. Using the very same principles and techniques presented in this book, Stacey took immediate control of her own destiny, creating the type of happiness and success she could only dream of. Originally from Toronto, Stacey now lives in California with her husband and two sons. She holds a B.A. from Wilfrid Laurier University in Waterloo, Canada. Stacey is also the founder of the Personal Development Book Club of America. Her motto is "You only live this life once. You might as well live it to the fullest!"

For more information, or to be in contact with Stacey, visit www.staceygrewal.com.

www.ingramcontent.com/pod-product-compliance
Lightning Source LLC
Chambersburg PA
CBHW031944090426
42739CB00006B/81